# No Sid

## The British Contribution to the Allied Victory in the Balkans, September 1918

Nigel Milne Birch
Student Number: 160330

Dissertation submitted for the degree of MA in Military History to the School of Humanities in the University of Buckingham

THE UNIVERSITY OF
**BUCKINGHAM**

October 2017

**No Sideshow**

**Nigel Birch**

© Nigel Birch 2018

First published in 2018 by Niroad Publications

The headlines and a cartoon in The Chicago Daily Tribune of 1
October 1918. The first of the four Central Powers has surrendered.
The remaining three forts are crumbling. USA never formally
declared war on Bulgaria or Turkey.

3

# Abstract
## Nigel Milne Birch
## 'No Sideshow':
## The British Contribution to the Allied Victory in
## the Balkans, September 1918

The British and French landed in Salonika in October 1915.
Greece, then a neutral country was the reluctant host. The
primary objective was to relieve Serbia from defeat, but the
landing was too late to achieve this. Other Allied countries
joined the campaign and fought over the subsequent three
years. Bulgaria, seeking to regain territory that was lost in the
Balkan Wars, joined with the Central Powers, and was the
principal enemy. The Allies were under the command of the
French, and Britain was a reluctant participator. Politics played
a major role in the conduct of the campaign. There were long
periods of inaction, and few battlefield successes. The British
wished to withdraw, considering that their forces could be more
effectively engaged in other sectors. At their greatest number,

there were over 200,000 British troops serving in the Balkans. There were many problems of a logistical nature, and difficulties with supply of shipping and establishing safe sea routes.

The Allies finally agreed to launch an offensive in September 1918, and a dramatic collapse of the Bulgarians resulted in an armistice within weeks. Within six weeks of this the remaining three Central Powers had each concluded an armistice and the First World War had ended. Although German war leaders wrote that the Bulgarian collapse was the cause of their defeat, historians have generally ignored that view, claiming that it was events on the Western Front that had determined the outcome of the war. A review of the historiography in this dissertation concludes that there has been little written about the Salonika campaign, and even less about the British contribution to the victory there.

This dissertation examines the role of the British in the allied victory of September 1918. It finds that although there was no immediate battlefield success when the British attacked, a review of the orders issued provides evidence that the attack was intended to be secondary and diversionary. The British were in fact able to exploit the subsequent Bulgarian retreat through the use of air power and turned this retreat into a rout. The result was that the Bulgarians requested an armistice within days.

This dissertation also examines the logistical challenges that faced the British throughout the campaign. Although some of these issues, such as the loss of manpower to malaria and transfers to other fronts did limit military capability, nevertheless, the British were in a position logistically to exploit the breakthrough when needed. A further examination of the British contribution in the areas of naval power and shipping finds that for three years the Royal Navy was able to keep supply lines open despite the menace of enemy submarines in the Mediterranean. The combination of these contributions meant that after the Bulgarian armistice, British representatives were able to negotiate an armistice with Turkey. As a result, the Royal Navy sailed into Constantinople, and the British Salonika Force occupied the former battlefield at Gallipoli.

This dissertation seeks to discuss these issues and add to the historiography concerning the victory in the Balkans in September 1918, and the effect of this on the ending of the wider war.

# Acknowledgements

I would like to thank the staff of the following institutions for their help:

The British Library

The National Archives

The Liddell Hart Centre for Military Archives, Kings College, London

I would like to thank Professor Saul David of the University of Buckingham for his invaluable guidance and encouragement throughout the conception and production of this dissertation.

I would like to thank the members of the Salonika Campaign Society, and their Chairman, Alan Wakefield, who led me on two trips to the battlegrounds of the Salonika campaign, and encouraged me to climb to the top of the Grand Couronné.

I would like to thank my wife, Tessa, and my family Stephen, Emily and Dawn for their support and forbearance.

8

I would like to thank my friends Ian Magee and David Metcalf, for their support and useful advice.

# Contents

# Declaration

I hereby declare that my dissertation entitled 'Salonika: the sideshow that ended the war': The British Contribution to the Allied Victory in the Balkans, September 1918', is the result of my own work and includes nothing which is the outcome of work done in collaboration, and is not substantially the same as any that I have submitted, or, is concurrently submitted for a degree or diploma or other qualification at the University of Buckingham or any other University. I further state that no substantial part of my dissertation has already been submitted, or is concurrently submitted for any such degree, diploma, or other qualification at the University of Buckingham or any other University.

Nigel M Birch     October 2017

Word Count: 24,411

Calculated in accordance with paragraph 3.61 of the Research

Degrees Handbook.

# Abbreviations

| | |
|---|---|
| ADM | Admiralty |
| BSF | British Salonika Force |
| CAB | Cabinet Office |
| CIGS | Chief of the Imperial General Staff |
| FYROM | Former Yugoslav Republic of Macedonia |
| HMSO | Her Majesty's Stationery Office |
| LHCMA | Liddell Hart Centre for Military Archives |
| RAF | Royal Air Force |
| RAMC | Royal Army Medical Corps |
| RE | Royal Engineers |
| RFC | Royal Flying Corps |
| RN | Royal Navy |
| RNAS | Royal Navy Air Service |
| SRS | Salonika Reunion Society |
| TNA | The National Archives |
| WO | The War Office |

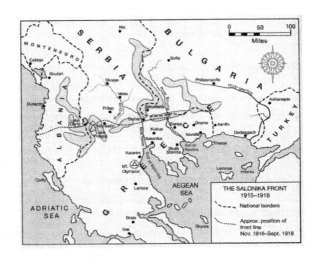

14

# Introduction

The Salonika campaign is one of the little known 'sideshows' of the First World War, yet it lasted from October 1915 until September 1918, a period of almost three years; the more famous and much written about Gallipoli campaign, by contrast, lasted for just nine months. Three of the Central Powers – Germany, Austria-Hungary and Turkey – sent troops to fight in the Balkans, but it was the little known fourth member of the alliance, Bulgaria, who was the principal combatant at Salonika. The geographic area of contest was known as Macedonia and this territory, previously part of the Ottoman Empire, was coveted by Greece, Serbia and Bulgaria. The Balkan Wars of 1912 and 1913 had ravaged Macedonia and left Bulgaria with a desire to recover lost territory. The decision by the French and British to land in Salonika in October 1915 was motivated by a desire to assist the embattled

Serbians, and to convince Greece and Romania to join the allied cause. Salonika was a strategically placed deep water port with a railway system that led to Athens, Constantinople and north into Serbia. It had been part of the Ottoman Empire until ceded to Greece in 1912.

In the event, the Allies arrived too late to help the Serbians who capitulated in November 1915. Little did they know that this would be the start of an unpopular enterprise that would last three long years. In January 1916, the French assumed command of all allied troops in Macedonia. The reasons were both military and political as the British had always recognised French special interests in the area, mainly of an economic nature. The British were reluctant partners throughout. Allied countries who fought in the Balkans included Serbia, Russia, Italy and, eventually, Greece and Romania. The commander of the British Salonika Force (BSF), Lieutenant General George

Milne, credited the versatile British with being able to play no less than fourteen different National Anthems.

The total Allied forces at Salonika numbered around 600,000, and at its peak in 1917 the British contingent numbered some 200,000. During the whole campaign, the British recorded nearly 500,000 sick and injured.[1] The number of British deaths from both battle and disease was 10,697.[2] The major contributor to illness and hospitalisation was malaria. The debate at the time, and subsequently, was whether or not forces of this size could have been more effectively engaged elsewhere. The fighting in the Balkans was always overshadowed by other campaigns, notably those on the Western and Eastern Fronts.

There were few military successes for the Allies until a dramatic breakthrough by the French and Serbians at Dobro Pole in the middle of September 1918 led to a general collapse on the entire front. Dobro Pole is a mountain on the borders of

Serbia and Greece, over 5,000 feet high. A Bulgarian request for an armistice followed, and it was signed on 29 September 1918. The Bulgarian armistice was followed in rapid succession by Allied agreements to end the fighting with Turkey on 31 October, Austria-Hungary on 3 November and, finally, Germany on 11 November. Writing immediately after the end of the war, General Eric Ludendorff stated in his memoirs:

August 8 [1918] was the black day of the German Army in the history of this war. This was the worst experience that I had to go through, except for the events, that, from September 15 onwards, took place on the Bulgarian Front and sealed the fate of the Quadruple Alliance.[3]

Field Marshal von Hindenburg set out his views to the German Imperial Chancellor in a note dated 3 October 1918:

G.H.Q. holds to the demand made by it on Monday, the 29 September of this year, for an immediate offer of peace to the enemy. As a result of the collapse of the Macedonian front, and of the weakening of our reserves in the West, which this has necessitated, and in view of the impossibility of making good the very heavy losses of the last few days, there appears to be now no possibility, to the best of human judgement, of winning peace from our enemies by force of arms.[4]

General Liman von Sanders, the German Commander in Turkey, asserted in his memoirs: 'From our point of view, the Salonika Army of the Entente remained a constant reservoir for menacing the Turkish coast and threatened our only land communication with Europe, our sole bridge to the Central Powers.'[5]

These German military leaders considered events on the Balkan front to have had a significant influence on the conduct and outcome of the whole war. Even if Ludendorff, in his memoirs, was by then seeking excuses for losing the war, Hindenburg, on the other hand, was making his report within days of the Bulgarian armistice. Despite this the Salonika campaign is considered, both at the time, and subsequently by many historians, to be a military backwater, of no importance to the overall outcome of the war. The British at home reviled the campaign as unproductive and inactive and the General Staff and Admiralty together represented to the War Cabinet, on many separate occasions, a recommendation to withdraw the British troops from Salonika.

A comprehensive report to this effect in May 1917, for example, recommended that all or part of the British forces should be withdrawn as soon as shipping could be provided.[6] The report concluded:

To sum up, it is lamentable to think that at the present time when the French Government hesitates to continue fighting in France because of deficient manpower, they and ourselves have over 400,000 men at Salonika who are unlikely ever to achieve any useful results, while an absolutely intolerable strain is being put upon our naval and shipping resources.

Despite these recommendations, and mainly for political reasons, the British remained in Salonika, and therefore participated in the ultimate victory in the Balkans in September 1918. However, this dramatic success was soon overlooked back home owing to the final surrender of Germany in November 1918 and the consequent celebrations following the ending of the war.

This introduction aims to summarise the relevant historiography on the subject and identify the key questions that have not previously been addressed by historians. There is a divergence of opinion and a varying lack of interest amongst general historians of the First World War concerning the importance of the victory on the Balkan Front.

*The First World War* by A. J. P. Taylor[7] mentions Salonika briefly to state that the war weary Bulgarians yielded almost at the first blow. Taylor also quotes Ludendorff's 'Black day of the German Army…', but conveniently omits the part of the quote that refers to the Bulgarian Front. *The Oxford Illustrated History of the First World War*[8] includes a chapter on the Balkans by Richard J. Crampton. His conclusion is that the Bulgarian forces, demoralised and weakened by food and ammunition shortages, easily broke in the face of the Franco-Serbian assault in September 1918. Any British input is not mentioned. Saul David's *100 Days to Victory*[9] purports to include the 100 key moments of the war across the globe. The Balkan breakthrough does not qualify as one of these dates. *The First World War* by John Keegan[10] hardly refers to concluding events in the Balkans at all, save only to state that on 29 September 1918 the Bulgarians signed an armistice. *To Win a War* by John Terraine[11] devotes two paragraphs to the final victory of the Allies at Salonika, claiming that it was pressure by the British on the Western Front that prevented Germany from propping up her Bulgarian ally.

Greater attention is paid to the events of September 1918 in *The First World War*[12] by Martin Gilbert. He states that the Bulgarian collapse was a blow to Germany and Austria, both of whom were suddenly cut off from all land links with their ally Turkey. The way was therefore opened for an Allied advance up the Danube, and in London and Paris there was great excitement at the thought of Germany becoming vulnerable through the defeat of her allies. He quotes Sir

Maurice Hankey, then the British Cabinet Secretary, who stated: 'The first of the props has fallen.'[13]

In *With Our Backs to the Wall*,[14] David Stevenson writes of the important events on all the First World War sectors in the year 1918. He gives a greater emphasis than most historians to the events on the Macedonian front. He considers that the Central Powers were wrong-footed and slow to respond. Hindenburg had stated initially that no reinforcements were available, as the Germans were fully engaged on the Western Front. As the situation worsened however, German and Austrian troops were found, but by then it was too late; the Bulgarians had asked for an armistice. The armistice with Bulgaria allowed the allies to sever rail connections with other Central Powers, and not only to threaten Turkey through Thrace towards Constantinople, but also to threaten to thrust north through Austria-Hungary, towards southern Germany itself.

Some historians choose to ignore the Salonika campaign entirely. Paul Fussell in *The Great War and Modern Memory*,[15] for example, writes only about the Western Front, despite the wide title of his book. He lists the other geographic sectors he intends to overlook - and does not even mention the Balkans. In similar character, Gary Sheffield in *Douglas Haig: From Somme to Victory*[16] devotes a single paragraph to the subject. To Haig, Salonika was a French folly that made no strategic sense, particularly as he was about to launch an offensive to relieve the attacks on the French army at Verdun. He wrote: 'All our resources in men and ammunition should therefore be sent to the decisive points, viz., France, and not wasted against Bulgars in the Balkans.'[17] Sheffield asserts that although Haig was militarily correct, he could not see that the Salonika campaign was sustained largely for the reasons of French domestic politics. Britain had to acquiesce for reasons of coalition harmony.

This dissertation considers the British contribution to the allied victory in the Balkans. Did the British effort deserve a greater recognition than was given at the time by either their Allies or the British public? Is the subsequent cursory treatment by historians justified? The study also seeks to examine the constraints under which the British operated in the Balkans, and how they were addressed. The study will aim to add to the existing historiography and identify omissions and inaccuracies.

There are some important secondary sources written on the campaign that will be referred to in this dissertation. The two volume Official History, *Military Operations: Macedonia* by Cyril Falls, is a major work. The first volume was written in 1932, and the second in 1935. [18] It is the second of these two volumes that is most relevant to this dissertation as it covers the period from Spring of 1917 to the end of the War. The period between June 1917 and April 1918 was a relatively inactive one in the Balkans, and it is therefore, the later period that occupies the greater part of the second volume of the Official History.

Alan Palmer's *The Gardeners of Salonika*[19] was written some 30 years after the publication of Falls' last volume. The book was motivated by the experiences of the author's father who served in Salonika for three years. The title is a reference to a sardonic newspaper article comment by the future French Prime Minister, Georges Clemenceau, who was a fierce critic of the campaign, 'What were Sarrail's [the then French Commander-in-Chief's] men doing? Digging! Then let them be known to France and to Europe as the Gardeners of Salonika.' Thirty-three years after this book was published, Palmer wrote *Victory 1918*,[20] a general history that usefully includes an entire chapter on the Balkans. Palmer emphasises that the Bulgarians were no longer enthusiastic for the war, and their abrupt exit knocked away the first prop that led to the final allied victory of 1918. He relates the British experiences on the battlefield, and credits them with strategic success in preventing the transfer of Bulgarian reserves.

Some forty years after Palmer's first publication, arguably the most outstanding account of the British military experience in Macedonia was published. *Under the Devil's Eye*, by Alan Wakefield and Simon Moody,[21] is a story of repeated failure on the battlefield by the British Salonika Force. The title is a reference to a Bulgarian fortification on top of the Grand Couronné, a heavily fortified hill overlooking the whole Doiran battlefield. The observation aperture in the stone fort was like an all seeing baleful eye watching the futile British efforts to advance. The book is written in narrative form with quotations from individual soldiers and war diaries. There are no conclusions drawn concerning the British contribution to the victory. The breakthrough at Dobro Pole, in the Franco-Serbian sector some thirty miles away, is examined in *Balkan*

*Breakthrough*, by the American author Richard Hall, part of a series of books on Twentieth Century Battles.[22] On this sector, the French and Serbians had built up a numerical advantage over the Bulgarian defenders, and within two days the retreat of the Bulgarians had become a rout.

The British Salonika Force's Commander was Lieutenant General George Milne,[23] known affectionately as 'Uncle George'. He did not write an autobiography, but his diaries are quoted in Graham Nicol's biography.[24] Milne, in his post war career, became a Field Marshal and the Chief of the Imperial General Staff, and he retained a strong connection with the veterans of the BSF. Reference will be made in this dissertation to a paper delivered by Milne on the Macedonian campaign.[25] The paper was presented by Milne in Montevideo in March 1939 at the invitation of the Uruguayan Minister of National Defence. This thirty page unpublished document is amongst

Milne's personal papers in the Liddell Hart Centre for Military Archives.[26]

A leading primary source is *Salonica and After* by H. Collinson Owen.[27] The book is subtitled, 'The sideshow that ended the war.' Collinson Owen himself was the editor of *The Balkan News*, the local British forces newspaper at the time. The book was written in early 1919, although a publication delay allowed consideration of the contents of Ludendorff's memoirs that are referred to in an opening author's note dated August 1919.[28] Collinson Owen considers that the statements of Ludendorff and Hindenburg, taken together, demolish all that was ever said in criticism of the BSF and lift the Force to its rightful place in the history of the Great War.

In the foreword to *Salonica and After*, George Milne wrote:

This book may help some to see in proper perspective how the crowning achievement of long and weary vigil in a secondary theatre of operations struck at the Achilles heel of the Central Powers and materially aided in their rapid collapse during the dramatic autumn of 1918.

Twelve years later Milne wrote an acerbic short preface to *Macedonian Memories* by Henry Day,[29] a personal history by Day who served as a Chaplain. Milne stated as follows:

After the recent flood of somewhat unpleasant war literature, mostly from 'the other side of the line,' the general public will no doubt turn with relief to a book such as this, which looks at war in the healthy British way. It often appears as if the authors of many of our war books were either temperamentally unfit for active service from the beginning, or else returned in a state which rendered them unfit to write about it.

Milne was, in 1930, a Field Marshal and the Chief of the Imperial Staff, and he was by then, possibly, writing from a somewhat impatient perspective.

In reviewing what has been written about the Salonika campaign, it can be concluded that majority of general historians treat the subject as unimportant. David Stevenson and Alan Palmer are exceptions. Martin Gilbert pays more attention but, after all, he was a former pupil of Alan Palmer. Apart from Palmer's *The Gardeners of Salonika*, there are only two other specific histories covering the British contribution that have been written over the one-hundred-year period following the end of the First World War. *The Official History: Macedonia*, and *Under the Devil's Eye*. It may be that with the arrival of the centenary of the Bulgarian armistice in 2018, an author is drafting a new work. In the meantime, *Under the Devil's Eye* has, in summer 2017, been reprinted in paperback for the first time. This unwarranted lack of interest by historians in the Salonika campaign in general, and the British contribution in particular, continues to this day and represents a gap in the historiography of the First World War that this dissertation seeks to fill.

Primary source literature, not unnaturally, tends to concentrate on relating personal experiences in the campaign. Historians have not written of any overall British contribution to the Balkan victory and therefore the campaign has drifted into obscurity as the years pass. Partially to address this matter, the then Salonika veterans formed a veterans' association – the Salonika Reunion Society – a few years after the war had ended. The Society was remarkable for the support given to it by its members over the years. It was also strongly supported by George Milne. He was the Society's founding Patron and was the guest of honour at its dinner as late as 1945. Milne died in 1948, but the Society continued its activities until wound up in 1969, having survived to the fiftieth anniversary of the end of the war. The Salonika Reunion Society magazine was called *The Mosquito*, an ironic reference to the insect that proved such a great enemy in the campaign. An article in the final edition of the magazine quotes from no less an authority than Sir Winston Churchill:[30]

The controversies which raged on both sides of the Channel upon the Salonika Expedition were silenced by the remarkable fact that it was upon this much-abused front that the final collapse of the Central Powers first began. The falling away of Bulgaria produced reactions in Germany as demoralising as the heaviest blows they had sustained upon the western front. The Salonika policy, for all its burden upon our shipping and resources, was nevertheless vindicated by the extremely practical test of results. This Bulgarian surrender pulled out the linchpin of the German combination.

An earlier edition of *The Mosquito*[31] had reported remarks made by the last French Commander in Chief of the Allied Forces in Salonika. Speaking in French to veterans at a dinner in London in his honour, General Franchet d'Espérey[32] stated that though the Armies of the East were often treated by the strategists of London and Paris as of little or no account, it was they who decided the result of the war.

George Milne had earlier had the opportunity to express his support to the British Salonika Force in an article published in *The Times* in 1928 when a special supplement commemorated the Imperial War Graves Commission.[33] In this tribute he reminded readers that final operations by the Salonika Force began on the British front on 1 September 1918. By 22 September (five days before the attack on the Hindenburg Line on the Western front) it was clear that as far as Bulgaria was concerned the war was over. The tribute goes on to comment on the uninformed criticisms of BSF that appeared after the war. Milne calls on the final judgement of history to produce the opposite of those hasty verdicts.

Falls, in *Military Operations: Macedonia*, however considers that opportunities were lost at every one of four stages during the campaign. He poses the question as to whether a decisive victory in the Balkans could have been won earlier.[34] The first opportunity was in October 1915 when the Franco-British forces arrived too late to save the Serbians. The second lost opportunity was in the autumn of 1916 when battle successes were not exploited but were sufficient to deceive Romania to enter the war on the Allied side. Romania was subsequently decisively defeated by the Central Powers in three months and then exited the war. The third lost opportunity was the unsuccessful Allied spring offensive of 1917. Because of this failure, the British concluded that victory in Palestine was more likely, and active operations in Macedonia were therefore ceased. The final opportunity that was lost was in the spring of 1918, as by then, because of the success of German offensives in France, there could only be a defensive strategy in Macedonia. It was not until the late summer and autumn of 1918 that the final, dramatically successful, offensive could be planned and executed.

There were two other factors that continually influenced the conduct of the campaign. Malaria was the first influential factor. This insidious complaint, although not necessarily a killer, had the ability to ravage a whole army and the same victim could be either weakened while serving, or admitted and readmitted to hospital many times. There were 787 recorded deaths from malaria during the campaign with 162,517 admissions to hospital.[35] The second influential factor was that of shipping. The supply to all the Allied forces in Macedonia was by sea, either a shorter route from the heel of Italy across the Adriatic, or via a longer sea route through the Aegean and up to the port of Salonika. Either way shipping lay at the mercy of enemy submarines based in their home ports in the northern Adriatic. The provision of merchant ships and their escorts became a major factor in the sustenance of the Allied forces.

The Balkan campaign extended over a three-year period. The varying political motives of the numerous countries engaged, and the many military and naval actions occurring make this a large subject. It is therefore important to clearly identify the areas that this dissertation does not seek to explore. This dissertation will not examine the reasons why the Allies first found themselves in Salonika in the first place, nor will it examine the politics of Greece's involvement, first as an unwilling host, and then in 1917 as an ally. It will not cover any analysis of the politics that existed between the British and the French or internal French politics. The French, who had overall command of the Allied Army, had considerable influence on the Balkan campaign. This area is the subject of David Dutton's 1975 doctoral thesis, 'France, England and the politics of the Salonica Campaign',[36] which examines the relationship between Britain and France at length. This dissertation will not consider the early years of the military movements in the campaign, the allied advance to the Serbian border in 1915, the subsequent retreat to Salonika itself, and the formation of the defensive ring known as the Birdcage around the city. The advance by the allies into the Struma valley and back to the Serbian borders in 1916 will not be considered, nor will the failed allied offensive in the Spring of 1917. In that offensive, the British were repulsed on the Doiran battlefield, circumstances they would remember when planning their next attack in Doiran in September 1918. This dissertation will also not cover the static warfare that took place between the spring of 1917 and the summer of 1918, up to the point where preparations were made for the final offensive of September 1918. The British were not engaged in the breakthrough at Dobro Pole in September, and this successful action will not be analysed in any depth, save only as to its consequences for the British front. It is not proposed to consider naval and shipping activities in the whole of the Mediterranean, but to only consider the consequences of any such activities on the Salonika campaign. It is not proposed to examine military or political events affecting other Allied countries. For example, besides the French, troops from Russia, Italy, and Serbia, were all represented in the Balkans. However, the British did contribute, mainly logistically, to supporting some of the activities of these allies. Finally, this dissertation does not seek to consider the Salonika campaign from the point of view of the Central Powers. Although the principal enemy was Bulgaria, the other Powers – Germany, Austria-Hungary and Turkey – all supplied forces and support.

Historians have downplayed the effects of the Salonika campaign on the outcome of the First World War. The British contribution has been treated in a similar manner and is often considered to have been futile. The lack of any famous British military victory on which to hang a tale has meant that it has been convenient to ignore the campaign. Any contribution made by the British off the battlefield has therefore been similarly neglected. The primary research question in this dissertation is to ask: What was the British contribution to the Allied victory in the Balkans in September 1918? The British were the reluctant junior partners to the French in the campaign and their contribution needs to be identified and considered in proportion to the difficulty of the tasks allocated and adequacy of resources available. An examination of the areas of British contribution will inevitably lead to the consideration of three secondary research questions.

Firstly, it is necessary to ask: How effective were the areas of British effort? The contributions were in the areas of army, air and naval forces, together with the provision of merchant shipping. Furthermore, the British were engaged in providing

41

support to other allies in logistics, supplies, training, and provision of infrastructure.

Secondly, it is necessary to ask: What resources were available to the British at the crucial times they were called upon to make their efforts? For example, there would be the question of manpower. At its peak, in March 1917, the BSF comprised of six divisions. By September 1918, however, it had been reduced to four divisions – one having gone to the Western Front, and another to Palestine.

Finally, it is necessary to ask: Did the British contribution deserve a greater recognition than was accorded at the time, or subsequently by historians?

# Chapter One

## The Contribution of the British on the Battlefield,

## September 1918

This chapter will examine the experiences and contribution of the British on the ground in the actions that took place in September 1918, the last month of the Salonika campaign, although later events will be included when relevant. The chapter will review the conclusions reached by general historians in the secondary literature. A review will also be made of other available commentary, and primary sources, published and unpublished. A conclusion will be drawn from the review of all the evidence as to the extent of the British contribution on the battlefield to the victory in the Balkans in September 1918.

The preparations for the offensive took place from July 1918 onwards, with the British Government finally giving their permission for the BSF to participate in the planned overall attack on 4 September. Different sectors had been considered as to where exactly the British attack was to take place. Eventually the main assaults took place on 18 and 19 September at Doiran and on both days the British, with the Greeks under their command, were bloodily repulsed by the Bulgarians. However, by 21 September the Bulgarians were, remarkably, in retreat from their unbreached fortifications. They were then pursued by the British, and on 26 September Bulgarian emissaries approached the British advancing troops. An armistice was then concluded on 29 September. The conclusion of a three-year campaign was dramatically quick.

The Allied Supreme War Council had met in Versailles early in July 1918 and had resolved that the Military Representatives (French, British, Italian and American) should report as to the desirability of undertaking an offensive in the Balkans. The report of the Military Representatives agreed on several important points. The material and moral state of the Allied armies had never been better; the moral state of the Bulgarian army was affecting their military power; and the other Central Powers could not bring effective aid to the Bulgarians. These factors therefore, combined to create favourable conditions for an offensive on the Macedonian Front. The exact timing of the offensive was to be left in principle to the Commander in Chief of the Allied army in Salonika, General Franchet d'Espérey.[37] The views of the British Commander, General Milne, had previously been asked for independently, and he confirmed his opinion that the Bulgarians were war weary and that an offensive could have far reaching results. He favoured an attack at the mouth of the river Struma where naval support could be engaged. He objected to an attack at Doiran because of a lack of men and guns, and considered that heavy loss would result there.[38]

However, General Franchet d'Espérey, had in the meantime issued detailed orders to General Milne, dated 24 July, with his instructions as to the participation of the BSF in the general offensive.[39] Key features of these instructions were that the British were initially to harass the enemy up to the point of the launch of the attacks on other fronts, and only after these attacks had made progress, were the British to make a general attack around Doiran. The BSF, which by that time had been reduced from a peak of six to four divisions, would have two Greek divisions under its command. It should be remembered that the British had already failed in the same sector in April and May 1917 and that the Bulgarians had had possession of the Doiran area for three years and it was strongly fortified. Milne promptly advised the War Office that the action envisaged would only be successful if he was provided with the reinforcements in the personnel, heavy artillery and the ammunition that he has previously asked for. At this stage, the

War Office replied that no reinforcements were possible and no offensive was envisaged before spring of 1919.[40] Sir Henry Wilson, by then CIGS, also reported to the Cabinet that he was averse to undertaking an offensive in the Balkans.

The impasse was resolved on 4 September when, at a conference held at 10 Downing Street, General Guillaumat, who was d'Espérey's respected predecessor, acted as advocate for the offensive. Guillaumat had previously been instrumental in drawing up the strategic plan. He had only been recalled from Salonika as recently as 9 June to help in France, because of the success of the Germans on the Western Front. Lloyd George, having been convinced by Guillaumat, announced that the British Government agreed to the offensive proposal.[41]

General Milne was then left with the problem that, although he had agreed that an offensive could have far reaching results, he was not going to receive the reinforcements he had asked for. He was also being ordered to attack a strongly defended sector which he had not chosen, and where failure had previously occurred. A major problem was that he did not have sufficiently powerful artillery to destroy the Bulgarian fortifications. In the absence of the desired 8-inch guns, he had asked for gas shells so that those bunkers could be neutralised by gas rather than explosive. After some pressure on the War Office, 3,000 rounds of gas shells (of the requested 15,000) arrived the day before the eventual attack.[42] The lack of a suitable calibre and type of shell would inevitably limit the effectiveness of the British assault.

The overall battle plan always envisaged that the main Allied attack would be at Dobro Pole, some thirty miles to the west of Doiran. The British played no part in this attack other than to supply two guns that were employed in the initial bombardment. The British role had been clearly set out in General Franchet d'Espérey's instructions of 24 July. Measures were to be taken to distract the enemy before and after the main attack had made progress and as such these were designed to keep the enemy guessing as to where the attack was to fall. The first such distractions took place on 1 September when a salient called Roche Noire was captured by the British in a two-battalion attack. This initial success served to deceive the enemy into thinking that the main thrust of the offensive would come up the valley of the river Vardar. The Franco-Serbian attack then commenced on 14 September and by 17 September the Battle of Dobro Pole was considered won. An initial gap of some eight miles had been quickly enlarged to sixteen. Hall, in *Balkan Breakthrough*, states that the Allies had achieved complete victory with a single operation in a short period of time. At no other time and on no other front did this occur in the First World War.[43]

The British then attacked at Doiran on 18 September, in accordance with the orders given, as the main attack at Dobro Pole was considered to have made sufficient progress. There were two assaults at Doiran, one to the west at the heavily fortified area where the Grand Couronné dominated the battlefield, and the other to the north of Lake Doiran, seven miles away. A success in the north could turn the enemy flank on the western heights, and this attack was led by the Greek 'Crete' division, under British command, and supported by British artillery. The northern attack proved a failure due to the solid performance of the enemy, a lack of adequate artillery, poor inter-unit communications, delays in the initial advance, and the reckless initial assault of the Greek infantry.[44] The attack in the west had the Greek 'Seres' division, again under British command, attacking with two British brigades. The Greeks succeeded in capturing the Petit Couronné (a smaller hill, previously much fought over), but the British were unable to achieve their objectives, particularly on P. Ridge, a 2,000 feet range overlooking the whole country to the south towards Salonika.

Taking stock on 19 September, the British assault was renewed with new troops and reinforcements to try and capitalise on the Greek success of the previous day. However, within a few hours, the Corps Commander, Lieutenant-General Henry Fuller Maitland Wilson,[45] had to inform General Milne that the attacks had failed and nothing more could be gained by continuing the fight. The fighting on 19 September won no new ground to add to the small successes of the previous day. Therefore, the next day would have brought new challenges to the exhausted British, if they had been ordered to continue offensive operations, but events on other sectors of the line happily meant otherwise. Because of the success at Dobro Pole, the Bulgarians defending Doiran were ordered to withdraw, and on the morning on 21 September the RAF reported that columns of enemy troops were to be seen retreating up the Vardar and Strumica valleys. The surprised British then prepared to pursue a retreating enemy. At noon on 22

September, an exultant telegram was received from General Franchet d'Espérey ordering that the Bulgarian retreat should be turned into a rout by an unceasing and resolute pursuit.[46]

The total casualties (killed, wounded and missing) in the actions described, in the forces under British command, were about 7,000, split equally between British and Greeks. The Bulgarians were considered to have lost no more than 3,000.[47] In certain British battalions, casualties were over 50 per cent of those in action. Three battalions afterwards were honoured with a rare distinction for British troops, that of having the French Croix de Guerre bestowed. A Victoria Cross was awarded to the commanding officer of the 7th South Wales Borderers.[48] Bravery had not been in doubt. The commander of the Armée Francaise d'Orient, General Henrys, who went over the battlefield some months later, declared that it was the most terrible position to assault that he had ever seen.[49]

The Bulgarian First Army commander, General Nerezov, was initially encouraged by the results at Doiran. He found his troops confident as the enemy attack had been broken. He therefore proposed that a general attack be launched against the British and Greeks on both the Struma and Doiran fronts in the direction of Salonika itself. A success could even relieve the Bulgarian front that had been broken at Dobro Pole. The Bulgarian High Command agreed; however, the Germans were unwilling to assist. The German Army Group commander, General Friedrich von Scholtz, had in his possession a copy of a telegram from Field Marshal Paul von Hindenburg to General Georgi Todorov, the Bulgarian Commander in Chief:

As your excellency is aware Germany is now engaged in a most terrific struggle on the Western Front. All our forces will be required for that purpose. I am compelled to refuse the request of General Scholtz that a German division be sent to Macedonia…In the present highly critical military situation the Bulgarian high Command must try to deal with the situation with the forces now at its disposal, and must reconcile itself to a possible loss of territory…[50]

The counter attack proposal was therefore dropped by the Bulgarians. They had first entered the war, believing that Germany would win, in the expectation of receiving territory. Their efforts would henceforth be better directed in withdrawing from the war as soon as possible, and on the best terms. The British, in the meantime, had pursued the retreating Bulgarians across the border into Bulgaria itself. British troops, the Derbyshire Yeomanry, were the first to set foot on Bulgarian soil on 25 September. On 26 September, Bulgarians under a white flag approached bearing a proposal to conclude an armistice, and on 28 September, Bulgarian peace plenipotentiaries were passed through the British lines and were escorted to Salonika. The armistice was signed on 29 September with effect from the following day. The entire negotiation was conducted by Franchet d'Espérey under direction from the French Government. The British were excluded, to their annoyance, but they would secure a certain satisfaction when reversing the position by solely agreeing the surrender terms with Turkey a month or so later.[51]

The British had therefore attacked as ordered against well-prepared defences. They had neither received any heavy calibre artillery, nor effective gas shells to deal with well protected stone and concrete enemy emplacements. The British forces had been weakened by losses from malaria, and furthermore a severe outbreak of influenza had occurred in August 1918. During September and October 1918, there were 12,000 admissions to hospital for influenza and 1,000 for pneumonia.[52] General Milne in his final despatch dated 1 December 1918,[53] reported, 'The effective strength of the

British troops at this most trying period of the year in Macedonia had, owing to climatic disease and a sudden and severe epidemic of influenza, fallen below one half of the normal establishment.'

The British, together with the Greeks under command, had been repulsed but nevertheless the Bulgarians had surrendered. What then was the contribution made to the victory?

Collinson Owen writes in *Salonika and After* that the British had made its contribution in preventing the enemy from mending the breach at Dobro Pole by bringing reinforcements from the British front. The result of fighting on the Doiran front was that no enemy battalion could transfer further west. Although there was no hope of the British attack succeeding, it was to be a sacrifice to ensure victory elsewhere.[54]

The casualties were very high, and the British losses alone were twice as great as those suffered by the French and Serbians in the attacks at Dobro Pole. However, Palmer in *The*

*Gardeners of Salonika*, considers that the British had, nonetheless, fulfilled one of its tasks and not a single Bulgarian unit that was in the line when the first attack was made fought on any other sector of the front. It was, unfortunately, a negative achievement, and the men whose courage had made it possible passed unnoticed.[55]

In *Balkan Breakthrough*, Hall wonders why the Bulgarians stopped the British and Greeks but collapsed in front of the French and Serbs. He considers that one factor was the defensive works at Doiran, and the other factor was the local commander, General Vasov, who was rated superior to his counterpart at Dobro Pole. However, Hall also asserts that one important success for the Allies was that the British and Greek attack prevented the Bulgarians from transferring units from Doiran to plug the gap at Dobro Pole.[56]

In *With Our Backs to the Wall,*[57] however, Stevenson introduces a note of doubt on the question of the British contribution. He considers that the attack at Doiran had proved to be an unmitigated failure. Furthermore, he writes, it was questionable whether the operation had even much assisted the main assault, and the Bulgars had retreated from Doiran because the Franco-Serbian attack was dramatically gaining ground. Writing some years later about Doiran, in a compilation journal of personal experiences in the war, an anonymous author considers that rationalisation of the British contribution is also questionable:[58]

No one can view the result of the operation as anything but a tactical defeat. Had it been an isolated engagement, there would now have been every prospect of disaster. The whole plan of the battle and every detail of its conduct are open to devastating criticism; but so are the plans and conduct of the great majority of battles. Luckily the Franco-Serbian advance was being continued with extraordinary vigour.

Before long, the Bulgarian army was cut in two and a general withdrawal began to take place along the entire front. Our Doiran battle was now regarded as a contribution to victory; for had we not been effective in pinning down the enemy reserves? British commanders are wonderfully philosophic, after all.

This view was challenged by correspondence to the editor of *The Mosquito*, from a retired Colonel, formerly a junior staff officer in the attacking British Corps. He refers to the article written by the anonymous Unprofessional Soldier, and points out that the complete strategic plan was based on the Serbians being able to scale heights considered impregnable. It was therefore necessary to launch attacks on the whole front. The tactical plans were made by the commanders of the attacking forces who knew the ground intimately. The sneer made at

British commanders at the end of the article was therefore due to ignorance of the facts.[59]

What were reactions at the time to the sudden Bulgarian collapse and how was the British contribution recognised? Contained in the Milne Papers in the Liddell Hart Centre is a message dated 14 October 1918 from King George V to Milne:

I warmly congratulate you and all ranks under your command upon the brilliant success achieved in concert with our Allies resulting in the surrender of the Bulgarian Army. I fully realise the hardships and unfavourable climatic conditions which have rendered the service of the troops especially arduous and therefore still more praiseworthy.

Similar messages of congratulation were received from the War Cabinet and Field Marshal Sir Douglas Haig in France, together with others from the British Commanders in Palestine, Mesopotamia, and the British Aegean Squadron.[60]

The reports at the time of the French Commander contain comment on the British assault. General Franchet d'Espérey's weekly report, dated 23 September and covering operations from 15 September, states that secondary attacks by the British and Greeks were carried out at Doiran. A footing had been obtained in the enemy positions and the Bulgarian reserves were pinned to the front in the region.[61] The next report, dated 30th September, however, is rather longer and contains full coverage of all operations. It includes two comments concerning British operations.

The tenacity that the British troops showed during the two-day battle of Doiran bore excellent results. The British air force largely contributed to the routing of the Bulgars and in turning their retreat into a disorderly flight, thanks to the

61

incessant bombardment of the Kosturino pass, entire columns of material were destroyed.[62]

This report of 30 September is four typed pages in length and contains, in the original French, approximately 1,000 words of text. In terms of emphasis, the British contribution for the action at Doiran merits twenty-two words in French with a greater thirty-seven words on the air force contribution. The latter will be referred to in Chapter Three of this dissertation. It seems from the word count at least that the report of the French Commander in Chief placed a greater importance on the results achieved by the air forces than the ground ones.

How did Milne express his views at the time? His private diary and personal telegrams to the CIGS, Wilson, show some of his frustrations.[63]  On 19 September, his diary makes sad reading. He had watched the battle. He entered, 'another failure'.  On 20 September, he informed Wilson that his divisions were only divisions on paper and not up to strength. Wilson replied on 21 September that although Milne may not have achieved the objectives aimed at, they had gone far to render possible the successful advance of the Serbians. On 24 September Milne received a message of congratulations from Wilson. However, by 4 October, Wilson is in a rather aggrieved mood, accusing Milne of thinking that he has been treated rather scurvily. He reminds Milne of the more important issues he has had to deal with in other theatres. Milne's command had therefore to be starved in men and material. Milne's reply refuted this:

I think you are under a misapprehension. I have always regarded the front as a secondary one and have purposely carried on with an absolute minimum for defensive purpose and never pressed my demands. As a result, the success here found the Army short in personnel for extended operations, a situation Bulgaria's surrender saved.

Milne's final report from Salonika, although dated 1 December, was not published until 23 January 1919.[64] A familiar form of words emerges, including the use of the word 'pinned' that is used in other reports on the same subject:

Accordingly, at midday on 19 September I decided to hold and consolidate the ground won. This included Petit Couronné, Teton Hill and Doiran town. P. Ridge and Grand Couronné had not been taken, but the enemy was severely shaken; he had suffered very heavy casualties, losing over 1200 in prisoners alone. What was even more important, the whole of his reserves which might have been employed effectively elsewhere, had been pinned down to this front and had suffered so severely so that they were now ineffective.

Twenty-one years later, Milne, then a Field Marshal, addressed a conference in Montevideo, and presented a paper on Macedonia. This paper was printed and a copy remains in the Milne Papers in King's College London.[65] As Milne never wrote an autobiography that would have included his Macedonian experiences, this paper is of interest. Milne concludes with his reasons for the Allied success and the lessons to be learned. There was superior generalship. Milne credits Franchet d'Espérey, and his predecessor Guillaumat, together with the Serbian General Misitsch in ensuring that the plan achieved concentration of strength and surprise at the weakest point of Dobro Pole. Milne also credits the French with the breach of that line, the Serbians with the successful pursuit, and the Italians and Greeks for fighting valiantly. The

British he credits with the magnificent tenacity of their attack on terrible positions which prevented the Bulgarian defenders from being moved to the threatened sector of Dobro Pole.

A further reason given by Milne for the success of the September 1918 offensive was the cooperation between the various Allies. Finally, the Bulgarians, though stronger than the Allies, had scattered their forces along the whole line and had no reserves ready to use. When the attack broke through, it was too late to rectify this.

*The Times* made its own contribution with a comment piece that appeared just before the final armistice with Germany. The Bishop of London had visited the Balkans a fortnight after the Bulgarian surrender and travelled extensively in the area. His letter dated 24 October 1918 from Sofia was published in *The Times* of 8 November. The Bishop's letter requests appreciation for the fortitude, courage and wonderful success of the BSF. He reminds readers that a large proportion of the army had had no leave for three years. Malaria and influenza had been so rife that even on 16 October 1918 there were 31,000 sick in hospital. He emphasises the beneficial effect locally of the conduct of the British throughout the campaign, and pleads for full justice to be done at home to the work of the BSF. *The Times* responded with its own tribute which, because of its relevance to this dissertation, is quoted here in full:

We publish today a letter from the Bishop of London pleading that in our congratulations to the British Army on its magnificent victories, the Salonika forces should not be forgotten. Few of us at home have any conception how much our praise, and when necessary our criticism, if only it is sympathetic, means to the Armies at the front - how much it sustains them in their trials and spurs them to fresh efforts for victory. In that regard our Army in France has been well served, and moreover its soldiers have had opportunities of coming back amongst us and learning how much they are in our minds. Not so the Armies in what have been irreverently called the 'side shows' - and most unjustly - for the firmest 'Westerner' is now ready to proclaim that without our Eastern campaigns his victories could not have been so decisive. These men of our Eastern Armies have had the dust and toil without the laurel of the race to victory. They have had few chances of coming home and renewing their enthusiasm in our interest and praise; their work – through no fault of the correspondents – has been ill reported; and too often the suggestion has been made that their work was all being wasted. Especially is this true of the Salonika Army. The Serbian Armies have done magnificently, but it is no disparagement of their achievement to recognise that it would have been impossible without the help of the British Army under General Milne. It is, as the Bishop of London says, not generally known that the initial success of the Serbian flanking movement was due principally to the success of the British on the right in making the enemy believe that theirs was the main attack. Moreover, after the Serbs had got going, theirs was, in fact, the principal attack so far as downright hard fighting went. It was, again, the British Army that first entered Bulgaria over the Belashitza range and into the Strumnitza valley. Add the malaria, and we begin to get some measure of the quality of the British Army in Macedonia.[66]

What then was the overall British contribution on the battlefield? A final exchange on the subject, in October 1918, took place between the French Prime Minister, Georges Clemenceau and the British Prime Minister, David Lloyd George. They discussed the recent Balkan victory as part of a lengthy exchange on the proposed nationality of an admiral to command Allied naval forces against Turkey in the Aegean. On 25 October Clemenceau (who wished to appoint a French Admiral) argued that the capitulation of Bulgaria, a victory under French command, was an essential element in producing the desperate situation in Turkey.[67] Lloyd George (who wished to appoint a British Admiral) responded with the not unreasonable point that the defeat of Bulgaria represented an Allied and not a French victory:

If you insist that the final defeat of Turkey has been largely assisted by the success of General Franchet d'Espérey, I am entitled to point out that these successes have been due to British, to Italian, to Serbian, and to Greek efforts in quite as great a degree as to the efforts of the gallant French troops on that front.[68]

The Bulgarians had decided in their Ministerial Council as early as 25 September to seek an armistice. They were mindful at the time of possible new threats from their erstwhile partners, Germany, or more likely, a conflict with the Ottomans who had been traditional enemies. Whilst the Bulgarian peace delegates were in no position to negotiate terms, in the event, the conditions that were imposed on Bulgaria were not particularly onerous. There were certain provisions that were particularly relevant to the Allied armies, even though they were no longer at war with Bulgaria. After all, there remained the three stronger members of the Central Powers, all armed and present in the Balkans and the war had not ended in this respect. The armistice provided that the Germans would have four weeks to evacuate Bulgaria, that the British and French would run the main Bulgarian railroads, and that no Serbian or Greek forces would enter Bulgaria.[69]

The Germans simply did not have enough available forces to assume control in Bulgaria, and they therefore withdrew in accordance with the terms of the armistice. In Serbia, together with the Austro-Hungarians, the Germans retreated towards the Danube followed in pursuit by the French and Serbians, the latter liberating their country that had been occupied for three years. Belgrade was finally reached on 1 November. Franchet d'Espérey then considered his armies could plan to march into southern Germany. Milne had previously received orders to cooperate with the French and Serbians in their operations against Austria-Hungary. However, on 10 October, a different role for Milne and the British emerged.

It became a point of political honour that a British General would command the Allied troops operating against Turkey in Europe, and a British Admiral would command the naval forces that would re-enter the Dardanelles. In the event, political compromise demanded that Milne's army that entered

Thrace towards Constantinople consisted of three British divisions, one French, three Greek, and detachments from Italy and Serbia. One division of British troops also went north to be represented in that army. Progress into Thrace was slow due to bad weather, inadequate naval transport and bad roads, although there was no Turkish opposition to speak of.

The armistice with Turkey was being negotiated whilst this was all happening, and this was effective on 31 October 1918, at which time the British were poised to occupy the Turkish town of Adrianople. In the south, the Turks had also been convincingly beaten by General Edmund Allenby in another sideshow that had been taking place - Palestine. The second prop to the Central Powers had been knocked away. The remaining role of the British Salonika Force was to be that of an occupation and peacekeeping force.

Those historians who have given consideration to the matter generally agree that the British had contributed to the Allied victory on the Salonika Front in September 1918 by holding down the Bulgarians at Doiran and preventing the transfer of reserves to Dobro Pole. What would have happened if the British had not attacked? It is possible that the Bulgarians would have been able to transfer reserves to reinforce the breach at Dobro Pole, and then continued to fight, supported by the other Central Powers. The Bulgarians were, however, by all accounts, by then, war weary, and were no longer expecting to achieve the return of territory lost in the Second Balkan War. The speed of the Bulgarian collapse was rapid, a matter of a week from 17 September (the date of the Dobro Pole breakthrough success) to 25 September (the date the Ministerial Council decided to seek an armistice). The events of 18 and 19 September on the British Front at Doiran would have affected this decision, and subsequent pressure by the British from 22 September and onwards assisted in turning a retreat into a rout. Milne's disappointment with the failure at

Doiran was recorded in his diary at the time, yet there was proper recognition accorded in the situation report for the week ended 30 September written by the French Commanding General. Inevitably, Clemenceau considered the victory to have been a French one when negotiating with Lloyd George. Although a secondary source, Stevenson,[70] has questioned whether the British effort contributed in any way, the weight of other opinions is that the British sacrifice contributed to the overall project success, and it had been planned in that manner. As Milne asserts, in his 1939 paper to the Uruguayans, the British should be credited with the magnificent tenacity of their attack on terrible positions, which held the Bulgarian reserves to their places. Doiran is the place where the main British memorial is located.[71]

George Milne also commented on the Bulgarian defeat in the special article in the War Graves Supplement of *The Times* of 10 November 1928:

The part played by the British Army in this battle was not spectacular and I have no desire to exaggerate its achievements. Its main task consisted of attacks with inadequate resources on an almost impregnable position. Its gains were, however, considerable and heavy losses inflicted on the enemy. The real object was not to capture ground...[72]

The consensus of the opinion that has been reviewed, both that written at the time and subsequently by historians, encourages agreement with Milne's own statements. The BSF had achieved the objectives that were set on the battlefield within the overall strategic plan. What then was the contribution made by the British in other areas? The second Chapter of this dissertation will consider how the British provided support to themselves and others in respect of logistical and other services.

# Chapter Two

## The Contribution of the British in the Areas of Logistics and Other Support Services

This chapter will examine the contribution that the British made in meeting logistical requirements in supporting themselves and, where appropriate, their Allies in Macedonia over a three-year campaign. It will be necessary to look at events that took place before 1918 as many of the logistical issues arose immediately from the initial landing in October 1915, and they had to be addressed in one way or another over an extended period of time in preparation for the final victory. Shipping and aviation issues will be considered in Chapter Three.

Although the fighting in the Salonika campaign was sporadic, and often confined to skirmishes and trench raids, nevertheless, at its greatest size, in spring 1917, there were six divisions of the BSF in the field.[73] In a paper to the War Cabinet dated 1 May 1917,[74] there is an appendix listing estimated numbers of both the Allies and Central Powers. The Allies at that time had a total ration strength of 635,000, and an infantry strength of 242,900. Within these numbers the BSF had a ration strength of 211,500 and an infantry strength of 80,500. On the other hand, the Central Powers are assessed as having a ration strength of 352,870 with an infantry strength of 238,000. The proportion of the Central Powers' fighting troops to total troops was, therefore, much higher than for the Allies (though the numbers facing each other was about equal). One of the reasons was that the Allies were made up of five countries, whilst the enemy forces were 90% Bulgarian. However, the report also refers to the fact that the numbers are disproportionate because of the Allied need to maintain extensive communications and supply lines, and that transport methods were necessarily labour intensive.

The logistical challenge is summed up by George Ward Price, an official war correspondent with the BSF, writing in the summer of 1917, well before the Bulgarian surrender.[75] He refers to some of the obstacles that the entire Allied Army of the Orient had had to overcome:

First and fundamental among these obstacles has been the necessity of creating, importing and improvising, in a mother naked land, the whole of an elaborate organisation which a modern army requires as a foundation to work upon. When you step out of Salonica you step into a virtual desert, roadless, treeless, uncultivated, populated only by scattered villages of the most primitive kind, inhabited by low grade peasantry. We found here none of the materials which modern armies need for their use, none of that machinery of civilisation which in France, for instance, lies ready made to the hand. Two roads,[76] in a condition quite inadequate to support heavy traffic, and three single lines of railway ran, at the most divergent angles possible, from Salonica towards the enemy's territory.[77] So that from the very beginning the Allied forces have had to build up slowly, laboriously, the whole of the system of locomotion necessary for themselves and their supplies - piers, roads, bridges, railways, - all have had to be created where nothing of the kind previously existed.

In addition to the obstacles referred to by Ward Price, it is possible to identify other areas where the British were challenged. For example, the medical facilities that needed to be provided in view of the sicknesses or casualties from combat. The existing maps of Macedonia were found to be inaccurate and therefore misleading. Wells needed to be sunk to provide fresh water. Local food supplies needed to be sourced or grown. There were substantial numbers of horses and mules to be looked after. Motor transport needed fuel and spares. The harbour facilities at Salonika were inadequate. The local labour needed recruiting and managing. The BSF was constantly starved of manpower and resource, and as an unpopular enterprise, from the summer of 1917 onwards, Milne was having to manage the effects of the demands on him to reduce numbers, yet at the same time to perform the expected tasks.

The subject of shipping will be considered in Chapter Three, but the logistical and other support service issues that have been referred to were all challenging ones, with the British having acquired varied skills and experience in addressing these challenges from previous campaigns. Logistical issues were continually influencing the major decisions that needed to be made. As late as March 1918, for example, a general scheme of contraction in Macedonia was being considered, involving a withdrawal of the BSF to a defensive line around Salonika. While the logistics of achieving such a possible manoeuvre were considerable, one of the undoubted advantages would have been the consequent reduction in the size of the front, and therefore its logistical and manpower demands.[78]

This chapter therefore examines in greater depth logistical and other support service issues and will seek to establish what the British contribution was, and whether it was effective. The chapter will also include a commentary on the contribution made by the British in respect of the social and other values that they brought to the Macedonian population. These influences were an important contribution to the effectiveness of the BSF.

The principal road that was established and maintained by the British was the Seres road that led, in a north-eastern direction from Salonika, across the Struma river and towards the Bulgarian held town of Seres. The road was approximately

50 miles long and the maintenance of this front was dependent on road transport. To assist, a light railway was constructed alongside the road for about 15 miles, but otherwise there were no railways in that direction. By December 1916, the Seres road had been completely broken down by use and bad weather, and it required tarmacadam to create anything like a permanent surface. This improvement was achieved with great skill by British engineers, together with the employment of Macedonian labourers, including women. Milne considered that the women of Macedonia were 'the best road makers and diggers of trenches I have known'.[79] The newly constructed Seres road was operational by the summer of 1917, although it was constantly requiring maintenance.[80] The importance of the Seres Road was such that it was referred to in a report made to the War Cabinet by the CIGS, Field Marshal Sir William Robertson, in response to an earlier criticism by the War Cabinet of the BSF's inactivity in the Macedonian theatre:[81]

The wide extent of the front held by the British Army, the roadless and mountainous condition of the country, and the absence of railways have made it necessary to carry out an abnormal amount of work on the improvement and maintenance of communications. This has been done with commendable energy. Four lines of railways have been laid, and new roads have been constructed in circumstances of exceptional difficulty, and throughout the winter some 10,000 men have been employed on the construction and maintenance of the Salonika-Seres road alone, which is the main channel of communication with our Struma front. [82]

The importance of the Seres road, and its maintenance, is emphasised by many contemporaries with experience of the theatre. The road, for example, is described by Collinson Owen as, 'the greatest artery of the British communications, bearing its daily burden of lorries and ambulances.'[83]   The principal architect of the successful BSF project to lay and maintain this fifty mile road was a Lieutenant-Colonel G. S. Pitcairn, who is an individual example of how the British contributed to the eventual success in the Balkans. Pitcairn was not a regular Army officer, but a former contractor who had made roads and railways in the Balkans before the war. According to Falls,[84] he was 'a past master in the organisation and driving of Balkan labour, and had learned from hard experience the quickest and cheapest method of carrying out any task set to him.' As a result of his skills and energy, by the late summer of 1917, the Seres road was capable of standing most tests. The success of these road constructing endeavours was repeated throughout Macedonia. The BSF took over, constructed, and kept under repair, 270 miles of metalled roads and actually made 175 miles of secondary roads and tracks.[85] The lessons learned in road making were also vital when the time came for the

86

exploitation after the final breakthrough in September 1918. Collinson Owen continues:[86]

The value of our road making experience was immense when the break-through came and we had to advance over the usual Balkan conditions of spongy tracks masquerading as roads. Our three years of hard experience in our own territory enabled us to have the proper men and materials on the spot almost immediately, who kept the communications patched up so that the men going forward could be munitioned and fed.

*The Salonika Side-Show* by V. J. Seligman[87] has its opening chapter on the subject of

the Seres road as the author claims personal expert knowledge, having lived as a supply officer in various camps by its side for nearly two years. Seligman wrote this history of his experiences in the summer of 1918 and they were published shortly afterwards in early 1919. He considers the Seres road to be, 'a pampered child on whom thousands dance attendance'. Writing of the importance of the road, reference is also made to the Royal Engineer, Colonel Pitcairn, whose contribution was so valuable.[88]

There was no standard rail system from Salonika direct to Seres, hence the need for
the road. At the time of the first French and British landings in October 1915, three important standard gauge railway systems branched out from Salonika. A fourth short standard line was subsequently built by the French. All the lines concerned the BSF to some extent, but it was the easternmost line that was the most important to the BSF. This line went from Salonika ultimately to Constantinople, but first headed some forty-five miles northwards to Doiran, before moving into Bulgarian occupied territory. This line was therefore used for supplying,

and communicating with, the Doiran front, although the effective terminus of the standard gauge line was earlier at Kilindir station, as Doiran station itself was within artillery range of the Bulgarians. The original pre-war railways did not have the capacity to deal with wartime traffic, and neither was there sufficient rolling stock. Furthermore, the railways were at first in the operational hands of the Greeks, who were a neutral country. However, in June 1916, as the Greeks refused to commit themselves, the railways were taken over by the Allies, because of their strategic importance.

There was, thereafter, a major contribution by the British in the areas of light railway line construction, the management of the easternmost Doiran standard line, and the resolution of rolling stock problems.

The trench railway system, using typically a 600mm gauge, (the standard gauge was 1,435mm), was commonly used in all the different theatres of the First World War, and was by no means unique to Macedonia. Many miles of these light railway tracks were constructed by the BSF. As the pressure on transportation by sea increased,[89] these light railways, one of fifty miles in length, were of great assistance to the Allies. Indeed, it was fortunate that the Bulgarians used the same gauge, as after the Bulgarian retreat in September 1918, it was then possible for the British to use the former Bulgarian light railway lines.

A large marshalling yard was constructed outside Salonika so that stores could be moved away from the congested port quickly. The shortage of rolling stock was addressed by various ingenious means. Wagons that had been sent by the United States to Serbia, and diverted to Malta or Alexandria as a result of the fall of Serbia, were re-shipped to Salonika. Obsolete trucks that had lain in sidings in Britain for years were shipped out for use. Sixteen main line and six shunting engines, made in America, were taken over from the Serbians. Their various parts had arrived without any working plans but these were successfully identified by British engineers. These engines were effectively the only ones in the whole of Macedonia that were not already out of date. Some of the light railway track that was laid came from the old defences on the Suez Canal, as the successful advance of the British across Sinai made this equipment available.

All equipment, troops, munitions, and material came through the deep-water port of Salonika. Virtually nothing was available locally. Unfortunately, the port facilities themselves soon proved inadequate, and at the onset of the Allied landing, British ships had to lie off the quays because there were no facilities for unloading. The British subsequently were only allocated 1,300 feet of quay accommodation (out of 3,700 feet in total). It was therefore necessary to build piers and connect them to the railways so that everything could be efficiently unloaded.

Ward Price compares the differing logistical problems facing the Germans in supplying their Bulgarian allies:[90]

The Germans load up a railway truck with shells in an Essen factory-yard and that same truck travels in perfect security over the best railway system in Europe without breaking bulk, right up to the Bulgar railhead, not a dozen miles behind the front we are fighting them on. What happens to a truckload of shells that we send out from Birmingham? It travels down to a port and is there transferred to a ship. Then it either starts on an eight-thousand-mile voyage by way of Gibraltar, with a good chance of being sent to the bottom by a submarine on the way, or it is taken over to a French port, discharged and loaded again onto a truck which crosses France to another port, where it is once more put on board ship and still has to face the dangers of torpedoing in the narrow seas of the Aegean.

In his paper given to the Uruguayan General Staff,[91] Milne refers to one of the major difficulties that the BSF had to cope with in Macedonia. After describing the difficult terrain, a series of mountain ridges placed at right angles to the line of advance, Milne then raises the problem of communication:

Communications were bad, except for the main Salonika-Vardar and Salonika-Monastir railways. No others existed.[92] All roads and railways had to be constructed. After a successful attack, pursuit appeared to be impossible, owing to difficulties in supply. In fact, the supply of the front line from Salonika was done only by cutting roads and building railways.

The capacities of the railway system, roads and port facilities were considered in a

93

plan for a possible partial or total evacuation. As late as May 1918, two senior officers, one British and one French, were despatched to Salonika. Their main mission was to report on the reduction of troop numbers in Salonika with a view to sending reinforcements to France. The British representative, Lieutenant General Woolcombe, was also instructed to report on the possible abandonment of Salonika. His report to the War Cabinet[93] includes notes on the subject of evacuation as regards the capacity of railways, ports and roads. The restrictions on these facilities were so dire that the CIGS reported to the War Cabinet that in the event of an attempted evacuation, 'it was quite possible that there might be a bad disaster to our troops in that theatre of war'. The debate on the subject of a possible British evacuation continued until it was replaced in July 1918 with the subject of an offensive.

The problems of communication brought up another logistical challenge that had to be addressed by the BSF. Given that Macedonia was such an undeveloped area, it came as no surprise to find that the existing maps were unreliable. These maps had been prepared pre-war by the Austro-Hungarian General Staff as part of a project that covered practically all of south-eastern Europe. However, the maps that covered Macedonia were particularly inaccurate. The BSF survey work started as early as January 1916 when a topographical section arrived, and eventually it was found necessary to begin a completely new survey. The BSF surveyors needed to start with new triangulation measurements over the whole British front, ensuring that these tied up with those measurements previously done by their French allies when they held those sectors. The exercise was satisfactorily concluded in the summer of 1917, when a new series of British scale maps was issued.[94] The contribution of the British to this important exercise was significant, because, quite simply, if soldiers did not know accurately where they were starting from, or going

95

to, then this confusion would not lead to an efficient military outcome.

A further logistical challenge addressed by the BSF was that of water supply. Outside Salonika itself there were no supplies of water by pipe, although given the nature of the terrain, with mountains, lakes and rivers, there was no actual shortage of water. However, the problem was that the surface water was typically unfit for human consumption. The BSF had the benefit of a specialised water-boring unit that had served in Gallipoli, and had been transferred to Salonika early in 1916. This unit was able to sink boreholes that then provided pure water, and indeed a special bore was sunk for the local brewery that supplied beer to the BSF.[95] The other Allied forces did not possess such equipment and wells of one sort or another were sunk for the French, Serbians, Italians and Greeks by the BSF's water-boring unit. A valuable extra benefit of this water production was that irrigation could be provided to grow crops for the use of troops – the so-called 'Gardeners of Salonika'. British engineers were also able to train the Greeks in water supply methods.[96]

The insect that is most closely associated with the BSF is the mosquito; while the animal is the mule. Mules were an important part of the logistical contribution as they were needed to deliver supplies to inaccessible areas. As early as July 1916 a requirement for a minimum of 10,000 mules had been identified. Mules were then sourced from Egypt, Cyprus, the United Kingdom and America. Muleteers came from the enlistment of Cypriots, Macedonians, Cretans and latterly Indians and they were supervised by British Army Service Corps troops. The dilemma was that mules were needed because lorries were insufficient in number and could not access inhospitable areas, yet mules still needed men to support them. They needed veterinary facilities to look after them, and shipping to deliver not only the mules themselves but also their forage. The importance of mules was so great to be mentioned in a report to the Cabinet.[97] The report explains why the proportion of support troops to fighting troops was so great. One of the reasons for this was 'the fact that the transport is necessarily pack to an abnormal extent, and thus absorbs an increased number of men for the increased number of animals.' Towards the end of the campaign, however, the number of mules and muleteers was reduced, with many returned to Egypt for deployment in the Sinai. The number of motorised vehicles in the meantime had increased considerably, with the British also providing transport to assist the Serbians.

There was constant pressure for manpower efficiency on the BSF, and the reduction in the number of mules described above was intended, for example, to save 3,600 personnel. As mentioned earlier in this Chapter, the BSF was at its numerical peak in the spring of 1917, with a ration strength of 211,500. There were then six divisions in the field, divided among two

Corps. However, after the military failures in the first battle of Doiran in April and May of 1917, the War Cabinet felt that the British forces could be more profitably employed in sectors elsewhere and therefore one division subsequently left for France and another for Palestine. Then, in the spring of 1918, the strength of the remaining four divisions was further weakened by a reduction from four battalions to three in each brigade.[98] Twelve battalions were thereby released as a matter of expediency to assist against the Germans who had broken through in France. The four remaining divisions, yet further depleted by malaria and influenza, were those who fought in the second battle of Doiran in September 1918. How then were these manpower shortfalls to be addressed? The Allies looked principally to the Greek Army, and there was a significant contribution by the British in the re-arming and training of the Greeks in order for them to participate in the final breakthrough battles, under British command.

As previously described, Greece had been a reluctant, if neutral, host nation from the time of the first Allied landings in October 1915. King Constantine had sympathy with the Central Powers, although the government, when under veteran Prime Minister Venizelos, supported the Allies. Matters came to a head in June 1917 when the abdication of the King was engineered by the Allies.[99] Falls summarises the position at this point, 'The division of Greece into two was ended. The Greek Army began, slowly but steadily, to take its place besides the Allies in Macedonia; and it's coming gradually transformed the military situation there.'[100] Greece, thus having declared for the Allies, began the slow process of unification, together with the training and re-equipment of the army as a prelude to taking its place in the line.

In December 1917, Britain, France and the United States each voted a loan of £10,000,000 to equip and supply the Greek Army; and in February 1918, an inter-allied military commission was formed to control the expenditure of this loan. The British delegate was the chairman. The Greek army needed to be completely re-equipped, and anything purchased in Britain or France needed shipping allocations, with consequent delays. In practice, therefore, a large proportion of the Greek equipment had to be supplied locally by the Allies. Broadly speaking, the British had the responsibility of providing food and forage for all nine Greek divisions, and, even at the time of the final offensive, the Greeks drew little from their own resources.[101]

In May 1918, the Greeks gained their first military success in the French sector at Skra di Legen, and by the end of the war it was estimated that Greece had mobilised some 270,000 personnel, of whom about 160,000 served in the Salonika war zone.[102] The British contribution, alongside their French allies, in supporting these numbers, was highly significant, as it enabled the release of British troops and allowed the Greeks to play their part in the final victory.

The contribution made by the British in supporting the Serbian Army was less significant, as that part was principally played by the French. It will be remembered that the Serbs were fighting to regain their homeland, and they participated in the breakthrough at Dobro Pole in September 1918. Previously, in early 1918, the Serbian Army had been significantly reinforced with the help of the British, and from an unusual source. Earlier in the war, the Russians had captured from the Austro-Hungarians a considerable number of South Slavs who now volunteered to fight with Serbian forces. British shipping and resources were able to bring two groups of these soldiers from Russia. One group sailed from Archangel before the port iced up. They travelled first by sea to Cherbourg, across to Italy and finally by sea and rail to Macedonia. However, a second group of South Slavs had to cross Siberia and were then moved by sea, via the Pacific and the Suez Canal, eventually arriving in Macedonia in April 1918. The British also had, from October 1917, a senior representative with the Serbian Army who was something more than a liaison officer. He was not placed under Milne's orders, but reported directly to the CIGS, and his role was also to keep the Serbians informed of the part that Britain was playing in Macedonia. This appointment was of value as it gained the Serbians' trust at a time when the British were reducing their military commitment to the Macedonian operation.

The medical challenges facing the BSF also need to be considered in any assessment of their contribution to the final Allied victory. As previously described, the major enemy was malaria and sickness, rather than battle casualties. The logistics of dealing with these issues were challenging, and included the transport and care of the afflicted, together with the subsequent rehabilitation of patients. In the BSF in the summer of 1917, for example, there existed 50,000 hospital and convalescent beds, of which over eighty per cent were occupied.[103] Experience showed that, even with plenty of care, over half the victims spent more than three months in hospital and convalescence. By the start of 1918, the Royal Army Medical Corps (RAMC) controlled four hospital trains, six motor ambulance convoys, thirty-one hospitals and five convalescent depots. In addition, at least twenty-four hospital ships had transported casualties to Malta or France.[104] However, the advent of unrestricted submarine warfare then prevented the transport of casualties through the Aegean Sea, and early in 1918 an overland route called the 'Y' scheme was initiated. This involved an overland route to the south of Greece, a brief sea trip across to the heel of Italy, and then by rail through France to Cherbourg and Britain.[105]

The BSF suffered more from malaria than the other Allied armies in Macedonia because much of its campaigning was done in the low-lying mosquito-infested Struma valley, rather than the more mountainous areas of Macedonia, where the other armies were chiefly located, were less affected. It was never established at the time whether resources were best directed towards the prevention of the breeding of the mosquito or the protection of the victim from being bitten. Admissions to hospital for June 1918, the worst month of that year, were proportionately less than those of September 1917, the worst month of that year, thus indicating an improvement in the management of the situation.[106]

In addition to their work for the BSF, the RAMC also assisted the Allies. The Greeks were provided with facilities for their own casualties, by way of transport and also by the provision of hospitals at the time of the final offensives in October 1918. The Scottish Women's Hospitals were not part of the BSF but were part of a civilian relief agency that was formed with the specific aims of firstly helping the war effort by providing medical assistance, and secondly of promoting the cause of women's rights. They were most closely associated with Serbia where they helped both the military and civilian population, and much of their work was spent fighting malaria. Their practical contribution and the psychological effect of their presence was part of the overall British contribution to the Allied victory.[107]

An additional, if unusual, contribution made by the British was in the city of Salonika in August 1917. A fire broke out in the Turkish quarter and, with a strong wind blowing, the flames soon spread to the port. The Royal Navy played hoses from lighters on buildings and refugees were taken away on British lorries. The original two city fire engines were small and antiquated, but luckily two new engines had arrived from Britain a few days previously, and were put into action by a British scratch crew. Ultimately something close to a half of the city was destroyed, including some ten thousand buildings;

there were 80,000 refugees, and for the rest of the war the city remained a ruined shell. The British helped by establishing refugee camps and evacuating the displaced population. A fulsome tribute of thanks is quoted in Collinson Owen: 'The refugees were led on the night of frightfulness and destruction with indescribable affection far from the flames and found themselves under the protection of an elect race whose name is spoken with gratitude by those who have been so greatly tried....' [108]

The reputation of the British and the conduct of the British soldier is a subject that is repeatedly raised in contemporary literature and commentary. Collinson Owen, for example, quotes Emmanuel Repoules, the Venezelist Greek Minister of the Interior: 'The British are practically worshipped throughout the whole of Macedonia.' [109] The Bishop of London, in his letter to *The Times*, wrote: '...the Governor-General of Macedonia endorses the opinion of the whole of Macedonia that the best piece of propaganda for the British nation has been the conduct of the Salonika Army.'[110] Milne, in an address to members of the SRS,[111] stated: 'You know you have a very great deal to be proud of, and I believe that what you did out there and the way you taught the people of the Balkans to behave, was appreciated by the people of that extraordinary country.'

The social contribution made by the British is the subject of a recent doctoral thesis by Rachel Richardson.[112] She considers that the pre-war values and behaviour of the British were not affected by wartime experiences. She concludes that the knowledge, customs and behaviours that British brought with them served as the foundation for the ways in which they coped with life at the front. She comments that on a global scale the Balkan Front may now seem both distant and insignificant in comparison to other historical subjects of Great War study. Yet in her view the Balkan front is an understudied aspect of the

Great War, thus confirming the central argument of this dissertation.[113]

Periodic reports were made to the War Office on the relationship between the French and the British under their command. The British considered that the French were capable of influencing other countries in their attitude to the British. A British liaison officer reported, for example, that French attitudes towards Greece and the BSF appeared likely to have military results, and political and economic effects that may outlast the war.[114] These periodic reports commented on wide ranging issues, and a later report, for example, commented on the Greek mobilisation: '…once in Macedonia, well fed, and distributed amongst British and French troops, these [Greek] divisions should improve rapidly and constitute a force of distinct military value for employment against Bulgars in Macedonia.' The report goes on to state, however, that, 'Greeks will probably never face Germans.'[115]

This chapter has examined the contribution of the British in the areas of logistics and other support services. The importance of some of these issues can be measured by the fact that they were reported to the British War Cabinet. It is possible to see, at this high level, references to apparently mundane matters such as mules. Milne routinely submitted a monthly situation report to the War Cabinet that normally included comment on matters such as railways, roads and medical issues. It is noticeable, however, that earlier versions of these reports contain more subject matter on infrastructure issues, than on medical ones. The later reports, however, are the reverse. For example, in Milne's General situation report covering January 1917,[116] reference is made to railways, road, docks and piers. The health of the force is stated as, 'good and there is no prevailing disease.' By way of contrast, in the report for April 1918,[117] there are no comments on logistical issues yet approximately forty per cent of a four- page report is taken up with the subject, 'Health of Troops'. It is therefore possible to conclude that as time had passed from the original landings, logistical issues had been successfully addressed by the BSF, but issues relating to health were still significant.

This Chapter has reviewed the challenges faced by the absence of facilities such as roads, railways, port facilities, maps and water supply. There were also manpower, medical services and communication issues. British support to the Greeks and Serbians has been examined, particularly in the areas of finance, training, provision of medical facilities and recovery work after the fire at Salonika. Comment has been made on the British contributions to social influence and the way they dealt with relationships with other Allies, particularly the French and Greeks. It is now necessary to return to the original research questions. What was the British contribution in the areas of logistics and other support services? How effective were the areas of effort? What resources were available, and was a greater recognition deserved than given at the time? The British managed to deal with infrastructure issues such as insufficient rail, road and port facilities. Despite limitations on men and materials sufficient improvement was made by the time of September 1918 to enable the BSF to mount the last offensive at Doiran and then to exploit the breakthrough. The British surveyed the relevant areas in Macedonia and supplied water and transportation in the form of mules and lorries. The BSF trained and commanded the Greek Army in the final offensive, and the British Government provided finance to Greece generally. The BSF contributed to the general morale and well-being of the local populace. BSF resources were used to manage medical and sickness issues that materially affected performance. The battle against the mosquito was not won, but it is able to demonstrate that was a reducing trend of sickness as the campaign drew to a close. The BSF manpower was limited, and back home the campaign was seen as a diversion of resource from the Western Front and other sectors, yet the final break-through was achieved because of the British contributions in the areas considered in this Chapter.

In Chapter Three, the dissertation will consider the contributions made by the British in the fields of aviation, sea power, and shipping.

# Chapter Three

## The Contribution of the British in the Areas of Aviation, Sea Power and Shipping

This chapter will, in its first part, examine the contribution that the British made in the Salonika campaign in respect of aviation. The second part of the chapter, a somewhat larger subject, will consider sea power and shipping. The two subjects, whilst not unrelated, are placed together for the purposes of convenience, rather than that they are operationally connected in any particular way. It was not until 1 April 1918 that the Royal Airforce, (RAF) was formed on the amalgamation of the Royal Flying Corps, (RFC), and the Royal Naval Air Service, (RNAS). The RAF was then controlled by the new British Air Ministry. Naval and shipping matters throughout the whole Mediterranean were controlled by the Admiralty and the Ministry of Shipping.

The British did not initially commit any air units to Salonika; by contrast the French were operating twelve squadrons of modern aircraft by July 1916. By this time the Germans had made three bombing attacks on Salonika by Zeppelin airships: the first on 31 January 1916, and the last on 5 May 1916 when the airship was brought down by fire from a Royal Navy warship and crashed in the Vardar river marshes.[118] By this time it was clear that a presence of the RFC was needed, not only for protection, but also for observation and intelligence. The first squadrons arrived in July 1916 from Egypt, but they were equipped with low speed reconnaissance machines that possessed no offensive quality against superior German aircraft. Therefore, the role of the RFC was effectively confined to that of reconnaissance, photography, artillery co-operation and bombing. Although improved aircraft types were introduced, typically the RFC planes were outclassed by their German opponents, and at that stage the experience in the air over Macedonia was similar to that on the Western Front. Furthermore, a German specialised bombing unit had been diverted from Rumania, and began, in February 1917, a systematic aerial bombardment of British aerodromes, camps and depots in Macedonia. These raids proved very troublesome until the unit was withdrawn in May 1917 for service against London.[119] In an attempt to counter these raids, the RNAS had cooperated with the RFC and provided fighters to engage the hostile formations, and bombers to engage in counter bombing.

The RNAS had its own ship-based balloon sections that were used for artillery spotting for bombardments from the sea by monitors. Only one such bombardment took place in January 1916. When the ships returned to Britain in May 1916, the balloon sections became temporarily land-based until they too returned home in October 1916, because they had been relieved by BSF Army balloon sections. Four months later, three RFC balloon sections arrived in Salonika and were used

116

to spot for artillery on both the Doiran and Struma Fronts. Though vulnerable to attack, either by enemy aircraft or by artillery fire, these balloon sections carried out observations until the end of hostilities.

A prime aerial opportunity presented itself in January 1918 when the modern German battlecruiser *Goeben* struck mines and ran aground off Nagara in the Dardanelles. The *Goeben* had been under nominal Turkish ownership since the beginning of the war, but was manned by Germans. She was returning from a sortie into the Aegean with her escort, the light cruiser *Breslau,* when both struck mines and the *Breslau* sank. To finish off the *Goeben*, and thus eliminate a threat that had existed for nearly four years, the RFC flew several bombers from Salonika to the closer island of Mudros, and from there they set off on bombing raids against the immobilised enemy ship and a nearby aerodrome. Bad weather hindered the operation, and a further bombing attack was planned for 29

January when it was discovered that the badly-damaged *Goeben* had been towed to safety and an opportunity had been missed. This incident, and the role played in it by the Royal Navy, will be examined again later in this Chapter. These two ships had always presented a threat to any merchant shipping that supplied the BSF, and the whole Allied Army, as they had to sail up the Aegean to discharge at the port of Salonika.

By April 1918, the RFC and RNAS had combined to form the RAF, and the fighter units in Salonika had, most importantly, been equipped with the latest type of aircraft. This meant that aerial superiority in the Balkans was finally in the hands of the Allies. It is therefore possible to examine the position as regards aviation from then until the final offensive of September 1918. Milne's situation report for the month of April 1918 noted:

Fine weather during the month has favoured aerial operations, hardly a day passing without our aeroplanes bombing enemy camps, dumps, railway centres and communications. On April 13, 21 of our aeroplanes bombed Hudova aerodrome [...] Two enemy scouts which attacked our formation were driven down and crashed. [...] During the period under review six enemy aeroplanes have been driven down, and over 14 tons of bombs dropped on objectives.[120]

Similar actions took place in the following months, and in preparation for the operations in September, a large number of reconnaissance flights were carried out, and a large number of photographs taken. A photographic map of the sector was prepared, comprising 1,250 photographs. Also, a large number of artillery registrations were conducted, together with further bombing raids on enemy aerodromes, stations and dumps.[121] In support of the offensive on 18 and 19 September at Doiran itself, several flights from the RAF were allocated to the two attacks on the east and west of the lake. The support provided was again of the nature of artillery work, contact patrols, reconnaissance and bombing. A balloon section was also allocated to each attack. The preliminary work performed by the RAF, particularly in the area of actual air combat, proved beneficial, as from the morning of 18 September, up to the end of hostilities, only one enemy machine was encountered, and this was driven down to its own aerodrome. As the officer commanding No. 16 Wing remarked in a letter, 'they [the German aircraft] must have realised that it was all up with the Bulgars and consequently packed up and cleared off.'[122] This absence of opposing aircraft enabled the RAF aircraft supporting the ground attacks to make their own contribution. Collinson Owen wrote:

During the battle, our artillery machines played an important part. Contact patrols flew over enemy trenches at very low altitudes, observers on reconnaissances watched enemy movements, and our bombers attacked trenches, camps and dumps with bombs and machine gun fire. Patrols were kept up throughout the day from dawn to dusk, and during September 18 and 19 no fewer than 272 hostile batteries were reported active and countered by our artillery.[123]

Despite the support given by the RAF, and as described in Chapter One, the ground attacks at Doiran failed. However, by 21 September the RAF was then reporting that the Bulgarians were retreating, their bases and dumps were in flames and the roads northwards were packed with transport and troops. This created the opportunity for the RAF to exploit the moment and to bomb and harass the retreating enemy. The only line of retreat was the road running due north of Doiran, through to Strumica in Bulgaria itself, a distance of some thirty-five miles. The Bulgarian Army would have been able to make good its escape unmolested, were it not for the threat from the air. Seligman was an eyewitness to the destruction caused in the bottleneck at the Kosturino Pass where he arrived two days after the Bulgarians. He wrote:

That they [the Bulgarians] did not retreat in good order is almost entirely due to the magnificent work of our Flying Corps. From the 22 till the 30 [September], when the Armistice was signed, our airmen gave them no respite by day or by night, ceaselessly bombing and machine-gunning the enemy troops on the line of march. Had it not been for them, I cannot see why the enemy should not have been able to reform farther north and offer us stern resistance. But this terror by night and by day proved too much for the morale of the Bulgarians - it was the last straw, and they rapidly lost any semblance of an organised army. They became just a rabble, each man fighting for himself. [...] In one field alone we counted nearly four hundred corpses. The whole road from Doiran to Strumitza was strewn with dead oxen and horses, dead Bulgarians, carts and lorries, some smashed, others left behind intact –everywhere confusion and the debris of a broken army. [124]

On 26 September, Bulgarians under a white flag approached the British bearing a proposal to conclude an armistice. The combination of events, from the breakthrough at Dobro Pole on 14 September to the routing of the retreating Bulgarians by the RAF, had ensured victory in the Balkans. The contribution of the RAF to this victory began in the early months of 1918 when aerial supremacy was achieved, and ended in the last week of September when the retreating Bulgarian Army disintegrated.

Although that Army was intact in the Doiran sector, having resisted the assault of the BSF, as soon as the retreat commenced, the RAF destroyed any future potential resistance. A similar experience occurred when the Bulgarians retreated from the Struma front where there had been no fighting. This was the first occasion that air power had been brought to bear on Balkan troops, and although General Todorov and his German allies had envisaged an orderly retreat, they had no notion of the havoc that would be created by air attacks on any slow-moving column that was caught in a rocky valley.

General Milne later wrote a note of thanks to the RAF Wing Commander:

I desire to thank you and all ranks of the Royal Air Force for the efficient manner in which their duties have been carried out since the commencement of active operations and to express my admiration of the skill and gallantry shown by the pilots and observers which have so materially assisted the success of operations.[125]

Milne summed up the part played by the RAF in his final despatch from Salonika:

The observers of the Royal Air Force reported that the Kosturino Pass on the Strumica road, the only line of retreat now open to the enemy, was blocked by masses of men and transport moving forward. The pilots of the Royal Air Force, flying low, took full advantage of this opportunity. They bombed the Bulgar columns and shot down men and animals with their machine guns causing heavy casualties that bordered on panic. […] It was at that time that the Royal Air Force found the Kresna Pass choked by the retreating enemy, whose Struma army was now in danger. Again, our pilots, as subsequent reports showed, did enormous execution.[126]

General Franchet d'Espérey also recognised the important role played by the RAF. His weekly report to his War Minister of 30 September 1918, written in French and translated for the War Office, read:

The British Air Force largely contributed to the routing of the Bulgars, turning their retreat into a disorderly flight, thanks to the incessant bombardment of the Kosturino pass, entire columns of material were destroyed. [...] The enemy has been ceaselessly harassed by allied aircraft, who have dropped more than 50 tons of bombs since the beginning of the offensive.[127]

In this manner, the British made a vital aerial contribution to the victory in the Balkans. The question of shipping will now be examined. The BSF's campaign in the Balkans has been viewed by most authors as land based. However, a review of the geography of the Mediterranean, and the position of the port of Salonika, will indicate that any land based campaign could only be supplied by sea, and this, indeed, was one of the reasons why the Allies landed at the deep-water port of Salonika in October 1915. The combined French and British naval presence in the Mediterranean was from that time substantial, but only the British merchant fleet had the capacity to supply the Allied Army. The sea route from Britain or France was through the Mediterranean and thence past the Adriatic and into the Aegean, with Salonika lying to the north-west in a gulf of the same name. A similar route could be taken by ships coming from Malta, Egypt, or through the Suez Canal. However, as the campaign drew on, all these passages became very perilous due to the presence of submarines, and an alternative route had to be devised that, as mentioned, was known as the 'Y' scheme. This involved a two-way flow, to and from Salonika, starting by rail, through France and Italy, a short sea journey across the southern Adriatic to Greece, and then again across Greece to Salonika. The reverse trip carried men who were sick or wounded, or going on leave. All the men and material of the Allies had to travel by sea, by one route or another, and the pressure that this created on shipping resources continued to be one of the reasons why the British were reluctant supporters of the campaign. The concerns of the CIGS, Robertson, and the First Sea Lord, Admiral Jellicoe, are reflected within a report to the War Cabinet dated 1 April 1917. The CIGS stated:

I would remind the War Cabinet that the Admiralty have expressed the opinion that    the strain upon our naval and shipping resources is becoming unendurable, and that, from a naval point of view, it would be less disadvantageous to have the enemy established at Salonika than to be compelled to provide the naval force and shipping required for the maintenance of our forces there.

A note by the First Sea Lord was included, and referred to the above statement:

I am most fully in agreement with the remarks of the CIGS. The strain on our naval and shipping resources due to the Salonika Expedition has been frequently pointed out by me, and I have also stated that we should suffer fewer shipping losses in Home Waters if the force at Salonika were reduced, because we could then afford to bring home some of the patrol craft. We could also afford more protection to Mediterranean shipping.[128]

The CIGS continued the theme, with a subsequent report on the partial or total withdrawal of the BSF. This would, he argued, husband shipping resources. A withdrawal of the BSF to France would, he said, save about half the amount of shipping needed in the Mediterranean; whereas if the BSF was sent to Egypt, the saving in shipping would be more modest. The report concluded with a recommendation that the BSF be partially or wholly withdrawn as soon as shipping could be provided.[129]

These pessimistic reports were prepared as a result of the losses that had been inflicted by submarines, both German and Austrian-Hungarian, based in the ports of Pula and Cattaro in the Adriatic, and also in Constantinople. These submarines could either be constructed in Pula or other Austrian ports, or supplied overland from Germany along with their crews. These methods enabled the submarines of the Central Powers to avoid entering the Mediterranean by the Straits of Gibraltar, as this route was long and dangerous for them. The submarines of the Central Powers were, as a result, highly successful: in the third quarter of 1916, for example, two-thirds of all tonnage sunk by U-Boats was in the Mediterranean. The situation got even worse for Allied shipping after Germany declared unrestricted submarine warfare in February 1917, and it was not until May the following year that the Allies introduced a system of convoys that helped to reduce the losses.[130] However there remained rich pickings for the submarines laying mines off all the various ports and channels leading to Salonika.

To counter the menace of enemy submarines emerging from their ports in the Adriatic, the Allies constructed a barrage across the Otranto Straits that, at a distance of forty-five miles, was the shortest point between Italy and Albania. In simple terms this barrage consisted of protective nets and was patrolled by light warships and drifters (the latter brought in and crewed from the British fishing fleet in the North Sea). The barrage was only partially effective and a raid on the line by the Austrians in April 1917 sank no fewer than fourteen of the forty-seven drifters. In the latter part of 1917, enemy submarines were once more travelling with ease down the Adriatic and into the Mediterranean.[131] The Ministry of Shipping produced a memorandum on the importance of recognising these problems:

It is recognised by the Ministry of Shipping that the Mediterranean presents special difficulties and that much energy and thought are being applied to cope with them. [...] The question of delay is of course intimately connected with the amount of submarine activity and special calls on destroyers for the transports of troops reduces the number of escort forces available for trade. […] It is feared that there are still some officers, Naval Military and Civilian, who do not understand that the result of the War depends on cargo carrying merchant steamers; and that the shipping resources of the world are being strained to the utmost to keep the civilian populations of the allied nations from starvation, while maintaining the supplies of munitions to the arsenals at home and the armies in the field.[132]

Enemy surface warships were generally contained within the Adriatic, however the chief threat that had to be managed by the RN were the *Goeben* and *Breslau*, the German ships already described. These modern ships had the potential to break out of the Dardanelles and, using their strength and speed, raid in the Aegean on merchant shipping bound for Salonika. The French, although they had the largest naval fleet in the Mediterranean, did not wish to take responsibility, and any British capital ships that were capable of containing the *Goeben* could not be spared from home duties or the risk of sinking by enemy submarine action. Therefore, the British maintained only two pre-dreadnought battleships in the Aegean, together with a number of light cruisers, to deal with this threat. The combined fire-power of both battleships was possibly enough to sink the *Goeben,* although the RN's main weapon was the laying of protective minefields. On 20 January 1918, the *Goeben* and *Breslau* finally exited the Dardanelles and sank two helpless British monitors who were moored within a netted anchorage in a bay off Imbros Island. Returning to the Dardanelles, the German ships ran into a minefield that sank the *Breslau* and damaged the *Goeben*. Despite a bombing attack by RFC aircraft, the *Goeben* survived and was towed back through the Dardanelles to safety. Yet the net result of this action was positive for the Allies – and had significant strategic consequences – because *Goeben* was so badly damaged it was no longer such a threat to shipping in the Aegean. This, in turn, allowed the Royal Navy to re-deploy some destroyers to the Adriatic to assist against submarines. Vice-Admiral Gough-Calthorpe, the Commander in Chief in the Mediterranean, reviewed the options that were available at the time and recommended keeping only a small force of destroyers off the Dardanelles.[133]

Errors had, however, been made. A memorandum by Eric Geddes, the First Lord of the Admiralty, and Gough-Calthorpe, describes the unfortunate series of mishaps that occurred in this incident. Prior to the exit of the two Turco-German ships into the Aegean, the two British battleships had been separated, one having unnecessarily conveyed the local commander to an appointment in Salonika. Then RN observers failed to notice the appearance of the enemy who, unmolested, sank the two monitors. Finally, there was the failure to exploit either by air or submarine the vulnerability of the damaged *Goeben*. It was only an unforced navigation error by the Germans themselves that had resulted in their arrival in a minefield.[134]

The Otranto barrage was strengthened in the spring of 1918, but its effectiveness continued to be questionable, and in 1918 only one German submarine loss could be directly attributed to the barrage. However, the convoy and escort system was becoming more effective: shipping losses were down, while the number of destroyed submarines was increasing.[135] Assisting the French and British in the Mediterranean were naval vessels from other Allies, Italy, Japan, Australia and the United States (who were never officially at war with either Turkey or Bulgaria). However, the major burden of the anti-submarine war was borne by the RN until the end of the war. A new, unforeseen, threat had arisen resulting from the success of the Germans in Russia. The treaty of Brest-Litovsk had been concluded in March 1918 between the Central Powers and the Bolsheviks (who had taken power in Russia after the revolution of October 1917). This had allowed the armies of the Central Powers to enter southern Russia and exert influence in the region of Crimea and the Black Sea. The future of the Russian Black Sea Fleet in Sevastopol was at stake. If the Central Powers got their hands on it, it might tip the balance in the Mediterranean. Milne was alarmed enough to remind the War Office that his force was dependent upon naval support. He reported as follows:

General Guillaumat, Commander in chief of the Allied Forces in Macedonia, recently requested me to represent to His Majesty's Government his strong conviction that owing to the advance of the Central Powers to the Black Sea, the naval supremacy of the Entente Powers in the Mediterranean might be endangered should the enemy succeed in obtaining possession of the Russian Black Sea Fleet. […] I am naturally unable to express any opinion on the purely naval point of view, but I desire to impress the dependence of this force on naval co-operation from the point of view of land operations. Not only is the line of railway communication through Greece to Salonika open to action from the sea but the right of our position is also dependent on naval support. [...] The evacuation of this position would react on the whole of the allied front line from the Struma to the Adriatic and might result in causing a general retirement along the whole front.[136]

One major consequence of the Russian Black Sea Fleet threat was the arrival of a number of large French warships in the Aegean, to add to the RN's two pre-dreadnought battleships. Although, in the event, no part of the Russian fleet fell into the hands of the Central Powers, the possibility caused a change in the concentration of naval power in the region. The French also considered that a strong naval representation on their part would improve their negotiating position post-war. The British wished to counter this tactic and, by October 1918, had the majority of naval vessels in the Aegean, and were, as a result, seeking overall command of Allied naval forces.[137]

The constraints on shipping and the dangers of submarine actions had a serious effect on the transportation of troops, both to Salonika and on returning from the sector, either sick or on leave. One of the major issues was the question of leave. Although the British provided a large amount of the shipping on which the campaign depended, it was a lack of shipping that prevented as much leave being given to the British compared to the French. In six months for example, from May to October 1917, only two British leave parties sailed for home.[138] Seligman wrote:

The French and British systems of reinforcement were different. The French automatically withdrew a man from

Salonika after eighteen months, gave him leave, and sent him on to the Western Front, replacing him with another man. [...] The British system was to keep a man out in Salonika until he was dead or dying. If there was still a little life in him, he was kindly permitted to go home to England, where, from the point of view of the Army he practically ceased to have any value at all.[139]

Collinson Owen asked, 'What use to send war-worn troops on leave if there was a high chance of them perishing on route?'[140] Three French troopships on their way to Salonika had already been sunk in separate incidents with a loss of over 3,000 lives. With the advent of unrestricted submarine warfare in 1917 this meant that some of the British troops would have been away from home for more than three years. The respite offered was the 'Y' scheme, that returned sick troops to Europe, principally overland, and this is the route that Collinson Owen utilised for his own leave after remaining in Macedonia for twenty-seven months. Questions on the subject of leave were asked in Parliament:

Sir M. Barlow asked the Undersecretary of State for War whether many men have served two years and even more in Salonika without any leave; and whether some reasonable arrangements for leave can now be made?

Mr MacPherson. Arrangements have now been made for the resumption of leave parties from Salonika to the United Kingdom, and I am hopeful that it will be possible to give leave in the near future to all those who have been abroad so long at Salonika without any leave. [141]

In reply to a later question, the Undersecretary had stated that, 'the percentage of officers and men who have been granted leave now and for the past three years from Salonika has varied from time to time, as it is dependent on transport facilities.'[142]

The RN operated a particular class of warship in the Aegean, and this type of ship, the monitor, made an important contribution to the support of the land forces. Monitors were basically floating artillery platforms, often with low draught, lightly armoured, but with the ability to provide big gun firepower to attack land based targets. The calibre of gun that was mounted varied from fourteen inches down to six inches, and likewise the size of the ship varied from a few hundred tons to six thousand tons. Monitors were used extensively in the First World War, and less so in the Second. In the Aegean, there were 11 British monitors recorded present in September 1918; the French had no monitors.

Monitors first arrived as the Allied naval presence was built up at Salonika, and two monitors participated in a bombardment of the Bulgarian coast in October 1915. They then protected the British line around Stravros at the mouth of the Struma. Over the ensuing years, Stavros was developed as a proper base for monitors who patrolled the coast looking for opportunities to fire on enemy batteries or trenches. Grove described in his paper how important the role of monitors was, as these targets could only be reached by naval guns. He also goes on to describe the part played by the Allied Fleet, including monitors, in neutralising the Greek Fleet in October 1916 and then ensuring that Greece joined the Allies. Grove wrote that this act was, 'a significant success of Allied gunboat diplomacy'[143]

In July and August 1918, two British monitors supported an offensive by the Italian forces around Valona, Albania, the far west of the Allied line. The monitors assisted in the bombardment and there was an initial Italian success to a depth of ten miles over a front of some sixty miles. However, the enemy, on this front the Austro-Hungarians, responded robustly, and drove the Italians back over the whole front, thereby causing the French to also withdraw their flank. The Commodore of the British Adriatic Force was at that instant concerned that the capture of Valona by the Austrians could upset the whole situation in the Adriatic and render the maintenance of the Otranto barrage impossible. This threat did not materialise and with the help of the British guns on the monitors, the sector stabilised.[144] The Italians did not participate in the offensives of September 1918. However, the presence of the British Adriatic Force was important as the Italian naval forces were considered ineffective. Furthermore, the Italians would not co-operate with the French, either on the land or by sea, for political reasons. Their sea based contribution was doubtful. A British RN officer wrote to a colleague:

Italy's share [of the suppression of the submarine] except in certain narrow circumstances is infinitesimal... Italy will offer nothing towards any sort of anti-submarine warfare we like to wage, defensive or offensive. If she did, her Navy is so inefficient that her assistance would be of little value. France has not a large number of effective craft for anti-submarine purposes, and though the French are eager to do all they can, they are on the whole incapable of running a sound naval campaign.[145]

Grove, in his paper, goes on to quote Captain Arthur James Mann, who is kinder to the Italian and French allies of the British:

Another and perhaps the most essential factor of all in the Allies' Balkan adventure was the remarkably efficient work carried out by the French, Italian and British naval services.

145

Only by their constant vigilance and co-operation were we able to keep down to a minimum those countless mine and submarine dangers that, despite due wariness, recurred throughout the Mediterranean, Aegean and Adriatic. Many minor engagements and individual acts of self-sacrifice and heroism in this service never received even the smallest passing notice in the press. These men, who contributed so much towards the Allies' final success, can never have justice done to them by any verbal tribute; nor do they expect it, being truly satisfied with the knowledge of having performed their duty.[146]

What were the contributions of the British to the allied victory in the Balkans in September 1918 in the area of aviation, sea power and shipping? The aerial contribution was that by the time of break-through, air superiority over the Doiran battle ground had been achieved. More dramatically, the RAF was able to harass the retreating Bulgars. This would have been a major factor in influencing the Bulgars to ask for an armistice. The British, having been constrained by a lack of quality aircraft at the early part of the campaign, had by September 1918 resolved these issues and were able to play an effective role. The major contribution that the British made in terms of sea power and shipping was to keep open the supply lines to the BSF and other Allied forces at Salonika. This was no mean feat at a time when the threat from Central Powers' submarines was actually increasing. At the same time the British were able to manage the relationships with their allies, the French and Italians, so that a form of co-ordination of activity took place in the Mediterranean. The *Goeben* threat was negated, if never resolved, but the influence of that famous ship was never as great as the submarines belonging to the Central Powers. The Otranto barrage was never effective. The RN contributed in safely transporting sick and wounded soldiers and also those

147

going on leave. Again, the danger of submarines meant that ingenious methods and routes has to be devised. The constraints on naval issues were that no modern capital ships were available to the RN in the Mediterranean, and there was a shortage of escorts and destroyers. At the same time the British merchant fleet was having to provide the substance of all sea borne transportation.

Did the British contribution deserve a greater recognition than was given at the time or subsequently by historians? The aerial contribution is scarcely mentioned in secondary literature. Moreover, while there were no dramatic naval victories, the British effort to keep supply lines open made victory in the Balkans possible.

This Chapter ends with a quote from General George Milne, in his article on Macedonia, the Salonika Army's Achievement and its contribution to victory, written for the War Graves Supplement of *The Times*:

My old comrades would not wish me to conclude without a tribute to the Royal Navy, the Royal Air Force, and the Merchant Service, so many of whom lie in our cemeteries, and to whose unfailing assistance the Salonika Army owed so much.[147]

# Conclusion

The conclusion to this dissertation will summarise the points discussed in the earlier Chapters, and will review the research questions posed in the Introduction. There will also be a review of the content of primary and secondary historiography to examine any relevant conclusions reached by authors, either writing at the time, or subsequently. In addition, this conclusion will address any key questions that have not been asked by historians, and to discuss why they have neglected the subject over the years. The conclusion will consider why most historians appear to have placed little importance on the victory in the Balkans in September 1918, even though it resulted in the surrender of the Bulgarians and the subsequent collapse of the Central Powers. Particular emphasis will be placed on the British contribution to that victory. What was the British contribution to the allied victory in the Balkans in September

1918? How effective were the areas of British effort? What resources were available to the British at crucial times? Did the British contribution deserve a greater recognition than was given at the time, or subsequently by historians?

In the celebrations following the end of the war, there were honours and financial rewards given to those British officers who had commanded and directed various forces, in recognition of their eminent services during the war. Lloyd George told the Commons, 'exceptional rewards shall be given to those who have borne exceptional responsibilities with exceptional success...our greatest difficulty was in choosing...'[148] Milne, who had led the BSF for almost three years, although credited with the ability to hold his army together ready for the opportunity in September 1918, was neither honoured nor rewarded. On the other hand, Allenby, the commander in Palestine, was the only commander of a side show who was rewarded, and Cavan, commanding in Italy, was, like Milne, excluded.[149] Questions were asked in the House of Commons as to why Milne had been overlooked:

Lieut-Colonel A Herbert asked the Secretary of State for War whether he is aware that Lieut-General Sir G Milne was in command of the British Army on the Salonika Front for three years and that this was an independent command; and whether, in view of the results achieved by the troops under the leadership of Lieut-General Sir G Milne, he will explain why Lieut-General Sir G Milne was not recommended for a reward like other Army Commanders? Mr Churchill. It would be invidious to discuss the reasons which guided the Government in coming to the decisions which have lately been approved by the House.[150]

Milne was rewarded by honours granted later in his career,[151] but at the time of granting financial rewards after the end of the war, it would appear that 'success' was not seen by the British Government as belonging to the BSF. In the immediate post war view, it may have been considered that it was only the success of the French and Serbian elements of the Allied Army at Dobro Pole that had achieved the collapse of the Bulgarians. Although Milne had fought throughout to sustain the standing of the British in Macedonia, the theatre had nevertheless been under the overall command of the French. Therefore, it was not only the military aspects of the campaign that were of importance to the post war British government when considering honours, political considerations also governed decisions. It is possible that Milne was overlooked for honours in order to prevent provocation of the French.

What were the opinions of the former German leaders as regards the importance and effect of the victory in the Balkans? Ludendorff and Hindenburgh both claimed that it was events on the Macedonian front in September 1918 that sealed the fate of the Central Powers. The German Official History is entitled, in English, '*The End of the World War on the Macedonian Front.*'[152] German authors such as Ludendorff conveniently blamed the Bulgarians for the collapse of the front, and even for the loss of the war itself. Unsurprisingly, the BSF is not credited specifically with any particular contribution to the German defeat. It was Bulgaria that collapsed rather than the Allies that secured a victory. Ludendorff stated:

We could not answer every single cry for help. We had to insist that Bulgaria must do something for herself, for otherwise we, too, were lost. It made no difference whether our defeat came in Macedonia or the West...The Bulgarian Government did nothing whatever to keep up the morale of the troops and the population or to maintain discipline. They gave free rein to enemy influences, and took no steps against any of the anti-German agitations. Entente bribery was the finishing stroke, even the troops that streamed back to Sofia being well supplied with enemy money. These, nothing else, were the true causes of the defection of Bulgaria from the Quadruple Alliance.[153]

The French celebrated victory in the Great War in a triumphal march in Paris on 14 July 1919. Troops paraded past winged figures set up on the Champs Elysées, each symbolic of a victorious battle. The only Macedonian names on the scrolls were 'Pogradec' and 'Skra di Legen'[154]. Remarkably, and despite Clemenceau's claim to Lloyd George of a French victory,[155] there was no mention of Dobro Pole in the victory parade. No streets were re-named in Paris and, as in Britain, no campaign medals were struck. Clemenceau had, before becoming Prime Minister, been a fierce critic of the campaign, he referred to the 'Gardeners of Salonika'. He had written, 'I continue to ask if several hundred thousand men, thrown into the East with precious materials, would not have profited us more decisively on the Western front.'[156] However, in office from November 1917, Clemenceau seems to have then concluded that it was too late to exit from Salonika. He may well have been influenced in his attitude by the arrival of the Americans on the Western Front, for possibly the manpower issue there was going to be resolved. Some of the British, such as Robertson, the CIGS until February 1918, and Haig, the Commander in the west, thought that the war would only be won on the Western Front, and side-shows were a waste of resource. The naval power and shipping that was necessary to support Salonika was also considered wasted. The detractors of Salonika were termed the Westerners. The new CIGS, Wilson, was somewhat less opposed to Salonika than his predecessor Robertson. Those who supported the continued Allied presence in Macedonia were termed the Easterners. Lloyd George, an Easterner, had steadfastly supported the BSF and he had authorised their participation in the final offensive as late as 4 September 1918. Joffre, then the Commander in Chief of French forces, had agreed to the original landing in Salonika and continued to be an Eastern supporter. The internal politics of the French, and the effect on the British is the subject of an entire doctoral thesis by David Dutton, previously referred to.

After the end of the war, the debate continued on both sides of the Channel. Would the war have ended earlier if more resource had been applied to the Western Front? Did the war actually end earlier because of the victory in the East? Or would the war have been won anyway, regardless of the victory in the Balkans? If Salonika had been reinforced, would the breakthrough have been obtained earlier and thus shortened the war? It is not possible to give an answer to these questions, merely to pose them and to present the evidence that the victory in the Balkans was important and the British contribution at that time was significant.

As reluctant supporters of the campaign, the British were unimpressed by the conduct of the campaign by the French, particularly whilst the Allies were under the command of Sarrail, who was eventually replaced in December 1917. British decisions were always influenced by the shortage of shipping. By the summer of 1917, active operations in Macedonia had been effectively reduced to patrolling, and two divisions of the BSF withdrawn. However, circumstances changed in the summer of 1918. Sarrail had departed and the Military Representatives to the Allied Supreme War Council had issued a report favouring an offensive in Macedonia, and as described in Chapter One of this dissertation, the results were dramatic enough to give justification to the entire three-year campaign.

Some of the primary source authors attempt to analyse the British contribution, even though these personal histories were written very soon after the end of the war, without necessarily having access to all the evidence that would become available with the passage of time. Seligman, writing in March 1919, summarised his views on the Allied contribution in Macedonia. He considered the numbers of troops tied up in the sector and the cost of sickness and problems with leave. He then wrote, 'Let us now turn to the more congenial task of enumerating our achievements. These may be summed up under six headings.'[157] The first point made by Seligman was that, the Franco-British actions gave sufficient support to the Serbians, who although defeated, were enabled to reform and provide a valuable army that participated in the eventual victory. The Serbians were universally admired for their fortitude. Ludendorff, for example, wrote admiringly, 'The Serbian Army had fought for years outside its own country, and had shown a brilliant example of true patriotism.'[158] The second point made by Seligman, was that

Allied actions had ensured that the Greeks turned from a hostile position to that of an ally whose forces contributed. Although the geographic position of Greece had given the country an importance out of proportion to its size, its participation as an ally was significant. The third achievement was that Romania had been influenced to join the Allies, rather than the Central Powers. Fourthly, the occupation of Salonika had prevented the Central Powers from securing a submarine base that would have threatened communications throughout the Eastern Mediterranean. The fifth point made was that for three years the Allies, 'pinned down' an opposing Army, which was numerically superior as far as front-line troops were concerned. The final point made by Seligman was that, at the final action, in September 1918, the Allies were in a position to deliver a conclusive victory. This victory enabled the World War to be rapidly ended. As his fellow contemporary author, Collinson

Owen, had stated in his work, 'Salonika- the sideshow that ended the War.'[159]

In the areas identified by Seligman, the British contribution is most closely associated with the two last points. The BSF 'pinned down' the enemy on the battlefield at Doiran. The phrase is used by both Milne and Franchet d'Espérey in subsequent reports. Those historians that comment on the battlefield performance, give credit to the British in the prevention of transfer of Bulgarian reserves to Dobro Pole. Even if this was to be considered a negative achievement by the BSF, it was, nevertheless, a contribution to the overall successful conclusion of events on the Balkan front. The British had addressed the logistical problems referred to in Chapter Two, and they were thereby in a position to pursue the retreating Bulgarians, whilst maintaining all their supply and communication lines. The BSF was the first ally to enter Bulgarian territory. The RAF successfully attacked the

Bulgarians when they were retreating and at their weakest, and the result was a request for an armistice by Bulgarian plenipotentiaries that came through the British lines. Throughout the three-year campaign, it was British sea power and merchant shipping that fought off the Central Power submarine attacks and delivered the men and materials to the battlefield. One of the effects of the Balkan victory was the collapse of the second member of the Central Powers, Turkey, who had concluded an armistice, effective from 31 October 1918. Collinson Owen, in the last chapter of his book, described how, on 13 November 1918, the British fleet lay in line off the Sultan's Palace in Constantinople. The fleet had sailed through the Dardanelles the previous day in accordance with the terms of the armistice.[160] The Gallipoli peninsular and the old battlefields, that had been evacuated by the British in January 1916, were occupied by a brigade of the BSF, a very significant, and symbolic action.

Milne himself, some twenty years later, when addressing the Uruguayans also claimed that it was the victorious offensive in September 1918 that struck the first knock-out blow to the Central Powers. He stated:

By the collapse of the Balkan Front, the enemy's whole front, even in the West, was threatened by a large encircling movement from the East. The first prop was knocked from under the German structure. The debacle once started spread rapidly. The moral effect of the victory was not less serious than its material advantages. [161]

Milne, presenting in 1939, had probably read Churchill's opinion on the subject as expressed ten years earlier in 1929. As stated in the Introduction to this dissertation, Churchill's views were repeated in the final edition of *The Mosquito,* that was issued in 1968:

The falling away of Bulgaria produced reactions in Germany as demoralising as the heaviest blows they had sustained on the western front. The Salonika policy, for all its burden on our shipping and resources, was nevertheless vindicated by the extremely practical test of results. This Bulgarian surrender pulled out the linchpin of the German combination.[162]

Whilst Milne, Churchill and *The Mosquito* agreed, the Westerners of Britain and France, post war, continued to deal the reputation of the Salonika campaign roughly and the argument was that the campaign had been a waste of men and material and, far from contributing to the final victory, had in practice delayed it. The result of these negative attitudes has meant the subject has been neglected by modern historians. As has been demonstrated in this dissertation, standard histories of the war dismiss the operations in the Balkans in a few cursory paragraphs, and some histories do not mention the campaign at all. It is not a popular subject for any new publication, and the last history entirely devoted to the subject was published in 2004. This account of the BSF's experiences was *Under the Devil's Eye*, by Wakefield and Moody. The previous comprehensive history of the campaign, *The Gardeners of Salonika*, was published in 1965, over fifty years ago. As Alan Palmer said then, 'Salonika was always good for a jibe: but where on earth was it anyway?'[163] Palmer continued:

With the lapse of almost half a century [from 1965] it becomes easier to see the achievement of the Armies of the Orient in perspective. Much of the old controversy seems oddly artificial, perhaps because it was fought over the wrong issues. No one today would seriously maintain that the defeat of Bulgaria by itself precipitated the collapse of the Hohenzollern and Habsburg Empires. The main German Army had to be vanquished in the field before peace could be assured, and that defeat took place in France. But supposing it had not been possible to breach the Hindenburg Line at the end of September 1918? ... Franchet d'Espérey's men were in central Europe because each of the allied contingents had performed the task assigned to it in the September battles...D'Espérey's offensive was a reinsurance against failure by Foch.[164]

Stevenson, a modern historian, wrote in the preface to *With our Backs to the Wall*, published in 2011, that his book grew out of a simple question. Why did the First World War end at the time and manner that it did?[165] All the war theatres are examined by Stevenson, and although the Western and Italian Fronts receive closest attention, he does refer to events in Macedonia as well as Palestine and Mesopotamia. He wrote as follows:

The process that began the First World War had started in the Balkans: so did the process that ended it. The Allied offensive in Macedonia launched on 15 September 1918 led to a ceasefire with Bulgaria on the 29th, and that ceasefire led on to Germany's request to Woodrow Wilson on 4 October to terminate hostilities…The Central Powers' unity collapsed with disconcerting speed. The ceasefire with the Bulgarians was settled in a rush: they did not consult their partners before signing…Bulgaria's surrender deprived the Central Powers of fourteen combat divisions, enabling the Allies to liberate Serbia and advance to the Danube…For the Central Powers, the implications of Bulgaria's surrender were all bad.[166]

This dissertation has considered the contribution of the British on the battlefield, and finds that although the subject has been neglected by historians, there is a general consensus that the BSF, although they failed to meet objectives, did manage to ensure that there was no transfer of reserves to the Dobro Pole sector. Hall, in *Balkan Breakthrough*, whilst referring to a Bulgarian victory, does also state that the British and Greek attack prevented the Bulgarians from transferring units from Doiran.[167] On the other hand, Stevenson is less convinced, 'it is questionable whether the operation even much assisted the main assault.'[168] Both Hall and Stevenson fail to consider one important fact that has relevance. The instructions issued by Franchet d'Espérey to Milne were explicit. The British were to attack at Doiran only when the attacks on the other front at Dobro Pole had made progress. Thus, the British attack, made under difficult conditions against a well-entrenched enemy, could only ever be of a secondary nature. The instructions to Milne from the Commander in Chief were outlined first in his general preparatory orders dated 24 July 1918. The orders to

168

Milne stated, 'after the launch of attacks on the other parts of the Eastern Front and when these have made a certain progress, attack with certain determination the enemy's positions east of the Vardar.'[169] The instructions are further expanded in more detailed orders dated 31 August:

The general offensive which is to be carried out shortly by the Allied Armies of the East is unlikely to bear all its fruit unless, after the period of the rupture of the enemy's front, exploitation of the success is undertaken without delay...The general offensive has for its goal the rupture of the enemy's front... A main central attack [will be] conducted by the Franco-Serbian forces...When this central attack has made progress and when it constitutes a threat to the line of communication of the Vardar, Anglo-Greek forces will attack the Bulgarian Army... As soon as the breach is made it must be enlarged by lateral thrusts to right and left…A vigorous pursuit will allow us to obtain considerable tactical results against the troops of the Bulgarians…[170]

Although the BSF did not obtain the breach referred to in the orders, it did nevertheless, and within a few days, secure the considerable tactical results demanded of it, that is to say, the collapse of the Bulgarians. The BSF action at Doiran only took place over a two-day period in a campaign of three years and whilst it is a fact that no breach occurred, it is argued that to look at this two-day period of fighting in isolation is incorrect. The overall result has to be taken into account, a pursuit took place, the Bulgarians were put to flight, and an armistice was rapidly concluded.

The British contribution in the areas examined in Chapters Two and Three of this dissertation are also neglected by historians. The contribution of the British in the areas of logistics and other support services meant that the BSF was in a position to exploit the Bulgarian retreat when it came, and subsequently the BSF and the RN was able to play their part in securing the surrender of Turkey. Had these facilities and services not been in place, then it would not have been possible to achieve either victory. Falls, in the Official Histories of the Military Operations in Macedonia, wrote of how the logistical problems were addressed by the BSF. Many of the primary sources also relate the individual experiences and challenges that were found in an undeveloped and malaria ridden country. However, secondary sources neither refer to the logistical and other difficulties, nor do these sources give any credit to the BSF for their resolution.

The contribution of the British in the area of aviation, principally lay in achievement of aerial supremacy over the battlefield at the time of the final attacks and the subsequent bombing and pursuit of the retreating Bulgarians. Had it not been for these actions the Bulgarian Army could well have withdrawn from the Doiran battlefront and regrouped. In the event, their army was broken by the success of the aerial pursuit, and within days an armistice was requested.

The contribution of the British in the areas of sea power and shipping was to keep open the supply lines and to support the BSF from the sea, despite the menace of submarines and threats from enemy surface ships. This support, both to the BSF and the other Allies, was delivered over a long period, from the first landing in Salonika in October 1915, until the victorious entry of the fleet into the Dardanelles in November 1918.

The author of this dissertation has been unable to find any study of the Balkan Operations in any Military Journal, or publication that concerns itself with anniversary articles of the First World War battles. Whilst there has been much written on Gallipoli, the Somme and Passchendaele, it is hoped that there will be subject matter generated by the arrival, in September

172

2018, of the centenary of the Balkan breakthrough and of the Bulgarian armistice.

The three areas of activity of the British that are described in the Chapters of this dissertation all eventually came together to contribute to the ultimate downfall of the first of the Central Powers. The headlines of an American newspaper at the time read, 'Berlin acts to Balk Ruin', 'Turkey begs for peace as Bulgars quit', 'Doom of Kaisers in surrender of Balkan Ally', 'Complete control of Bulgaria given to Allied Armies'.[171] The headline writer's art is to summarise an article in a way that attracts a reader. Events in the Balkans and their effect on the outcome of the First World War were soon overtaken by other headlines. The breakthrough in the Balkans was therefore quickly forgotten and has been subsequently neglected by historians. However, it is hoped that further debate will continue, and this dissertation will add to the subject by its presentation of the British contribution to the victory in the Balkans in September 1918.

# BIBLIOGRAPHY

## PRIMARY SOURCES, UNPUBLISHED

### Official Documents

The National Archives (TNA), London:

ADM 116/1420: Memorandum by Ministry of Shipping on merchant ships

ADM 116/1807: Memorandum regarding The *Goeben*

ADM 116/1809: Shipping Losses

ADM 116/1810: Admiralty to Cabinet regarding command in Aegean

ADM 137/1580: Reliance of BSF on shipping

ADM 137/2180: Negotiations with Turkey and role of the French

CAB 23/1/31: Difficulties of Shipping

CAB 24/6/5: French Attitudes

CAB 24/6/13: Milne Report on Railways

CAB 24/8/50: Lack of Co-operation between Allies

CAB 24/9/48: Cabinet Review of Situation at Salonika

CAB 24/12/6: Withdrawal of British from Salonika

CAB 24/13/77: Reduction of Forces at Salonika

CAB 24/26/40: British forces quality compared to other Allies

CAB 24/32/87: Attitude of the French

CAB 24/47/72: Comments on Serbians and Greeks

CAB 24/51/66: Milne situation report for April 1918

CAB 24/51/95: Loan to Greece

CAB 25/25: Possibility of Retreat from front to Salonika

CAB 25/34: Possibility of Evacuation of Salonika and Railway capacity

CAB 25/101: Replacement of British Troops by Indian Forces

CAB 45/3: Operations of the Salonika Force 1916-1918

FO 286/682/694: Salonika: appreciation of British Army

FO 286/679: Reorganisation of Greek Army, provision of rolling stock, supplies and materials

MSS F/52/2/43: Lloyd George Papers, Correspondence from Clemenceau

MSS F/50/3/39: Lloyd George Papers, Correspondence to Clemenceau

WO 158/756: History of the British Salonika Army

WO 158/763: Offensive operations correspondence

WO 106/1367: Situation and Operation Reports July-September 1918

WO 106/1385: Proposals for an offensive in the Balkans

WO 106/1386: Strength of British Forces and proposal to replace British Units by Indian Troops

British Library (BL), London:

Collection 425/1460: Colonel Barge's report on his third tour of the Balkan front, 1918
Collection NPL FMISC86: The *Balkan News*, various editions

<u>Private Papers</u>

Liddell Hart Centre for Military Archives (LHCMA), Kings College, London:
Field Marshal George F. Milne Papers

PRIMARY SOURCES, PUBLISHED

Baines, Andrew, and Joanna Palmer, eds, *Dearest Mother: First World War Letters Home from a Young Sapper Officer in France and Salonika* (Solihull: Helion & Company, 2015)
Collinson Owen, Harry, *Salonica and After* (London: Hodder & Stoughton, 1919)

Day, Henry C., *Macedonian Memories* (London: H. Cranton, 1930)

Freemantle, Sydney, *My Naval Career* (London: Hutchinson, 1949)

Ludendorff, Erich, *Ludendorff's Own Story, August 1914-November 1918,* Vol. II, (London: Hutchinson, 1919; repr. 2015)

Mann, Arthur James, *The Salonika Front* (London: A & C Black, 1920)

Packer, Charles, *Return to Salonika* (London: Cassell, 1964)

Rutter, Owen, *Tiadatha* (London: Philip Allen, 1935)

Sanders, Liman von, *Five Years in Turkey* (Annapolis: US Naval Institute, 1927)

Sandes, Flora, *The Autobiography of a Woman Soldier: A Brief Record of Adventure with the Serbian Army,* (New York: Frederick A. Stokes, 1927)

Seligman, Vincent Julian, *The Salonica Side-Show* (London: G. Allen & Unwin, 1919)

Ward Price, George, *The Story of the Salonica Army* (London: Hodder & Stoughton, 1918)

## SECONDARY SOURCES

<u>Books</u>

Chatterton, E. Keble, *Seas of Adventures* (London: Hurst & Blackett, 1936)

Crampton, Richard J., 'The Balkans, 1914-1918', in *The Oxford Illustrated History of the First World War*, ed. by Hew Strachan (Oxford: Oxford University Press, 1998)

David, Saul, *100 Days to Victory: How the Great War Was Fought and Won 1914-1918* (London: Hodder & Stoughton, 2013)

Dieterich, D., *Weltkreigsende an Der Mazedonischen Front* (Berlin: Gerhard Stalling, 1928)

Falls, Cyril, *Military Operations: Macedonia*, 2 vols (London: HMSO, 1932-1935; repr. 2015)

Fussell, Paul, *The Great War and Modern Memory* (Oxford: Oxford University Press, 2000)

Gilbert, Martin, *The First World War* (New York: Henry Holt, 1994)

Hall, Richard C., *Balkan Breakthrough: The Battle of Dobro Pole 1918* (Bloomington: Indiana University Press, 2010)

Halpern, Paul G., *The Royal Navy in the Mediterranean, 1915-18* (Aldershot: Temple Smith, 1987)

Halpern, Paul G., *A Naval History of World War 1* (Annapolis: US Naval Institute, 1994).

Keegan, John, *The First World War* (London: Hutchinson, 1998)

Macpherson, William, and Thomas Mitchell, *History of the Great War Medical Services*, 4 vols, (London: HMSO, 1921-4)

Nicol, Graham, *Uncle George: Biography of Field Marshal Lord Milne of Salonika and Rubislaw* (London: Reedminster Publications, 1976)

Palmer, Alan, *The Gardeners of Salonika* (London: Faber and Faber, 1965)

Palmer, Alan, *Victory 1918* (London: Weidenfield & Nicholson, 1998)

Sheffield, Gary, *Douglas Haig: From the Somme to Victory* (London: Aurum Press, 2011)

Stevenson, David, *With Our Backs to the Wall* (London: Allen Lane, 2011)

Taylor, A. J. P., *The First World War: An Illustrated History* (London: Hamish Hamilton, 1963)

Terraine, John, *To Win A War: 1918, the Year of Victory* (London: Sidgwick and Jackson, 1978)

Usborne, Cecil, *Blast and Counterblast: A Naval Impression of the War* (London: John Murray, 1935)

Wakefield, Alan, and Simon Moody, *Under the Devil's Eye: The British Military Experience in Macedonia 1915-18* (Stroud: Sutton Publishing, 2004; repr. 2011

Chapters, Journals and Newspapers

Anon., 'An Unprofessional Soldier' and 'I saw the Futile Massacre at Doiran', in John Hammerton, ed., *The Great War: I Was There* (London: Amalgamated Press, 1938)

Reproduction of the Bulgarian Armistice Convention, September 1918, *American Journal of International Law*, 12/4 (October 1919), 402-4

Burns, Ian, 'HMS Canning and 7KBS at Salonika', *The New Mosquito*, 35 (April 2017), 6-19

*Hansard*, Commons debates of 24 July 1918, 1 August 1918, 11 August 1919

Mendes, Stephen and Alan Cumming, 'The Scottish Women's Hospitals for Foreign Service', *The New Mosquito*, 33 (April 2016) 6-11

*The Mosquito*, September 1937, September 1945, December 1968 (Editorials and Correspondence)

*The Times*, 8 November 1918, 23 January 1919, 22 August 1919 (Editorials), 10 November 1928

## Unpublished Conference Papers

Grove, Eric, 'Salonika and Macedonia: The Vital Maritime Dimension' (unpublished paper, given at the International Conference on The Salonika Front in World War One, Thessaloniki, 22-24 October 2015).

## Unpublished Theses

Dutton, David, 'France, England and the Politics of the Salonica Campaign' (doctoral thesis, University College, London, 1975)

Perkins, James Andrew, 'British liberalism and the Balkans, c. 1875- 1925' (doctoral thesis, Birkbeck, University of London, 2014)

Richardson, Rachel, 'Home away from the home front: the British in the Balkans during the Great War' (doctoral thesis, Birkbeck, University of London, 2014)

# ENDNOTES

[1] Cyril Falls, *Military Operations: Macedonia - Volume II: From the Spring of 1917 to the End of the War,* 2 vols (London: HMSO, 1935), II, 351-2.

[2] As commemorated on the memorial to the British Salonika Forces at Doiran, erected in 1926. Falls quotes a total of 9,424, if missing are included.

[3] Erich Ludendorff, *Ludendorff's Own Story: August 1914-November 1918,* 2 vols (London: Hutchinson, 1919), II, 679.

[4] Ludendorff, II, 729.

[5] Liman von Sanders, *Five Years in Turkey* (Annapolis: US Naval Institute, 1927), p. 101.

[6] Report to the War Cabinet by Field-Marshal W. R. Robertson, CIGS, dated 1 May 1917, London, The National Archives (TNA), CAB 24/12/006.

[7] A. J. P. Taylor, *The First World War: An Illustrated History* (London: Hamish Hamilton, 1963).

[8] Richard J. Crampton, 'The Balkans 1914-1918', in *The Oxford Illustrated History of the First World War,* ed. by Hew Strachan (Oxford: Oxford University Press, 1998).

[9] Saul David, *100 Days to Victory: How the Great War Was Fought and Won* (London: Hodder & Stoughton, 2013).

[10] John Keegan, *The First World War* (London: Hutchinson, 1998).

[11] John Terraine, *To Win A War: 1918, the Year of Victory* (London: Sidgwick and Jackson, 1978).

[12] Martin Gilbert, *The First World War* (New York: Henry Holt, 1994).

[13] Gilbert, p. 468.

[14] David Stevenson, *With Our Backs to the Wall* (London: Allen Lane, 2011).

[15] Paul Fussell, *The Great War and Modern Memory* (Oxford: Oxford University Press, 2000).

[16] Gary Sheffield, *Douglas Haig: From the Somme to Victory* (London: Aurum Press, 2011).

[17] Sheffield, p. 165.

[18] Cyril Falls, *Military Operations: Macedonia*, 2 vols (London: HMSO, 1932-5)

[19] Alan Palmer, *The Gardeners of Salonika* (London: Faber and Faber, 1965).

[20] Alan Palmer, *Victory 1918* (London: Weidenfield & Nicholson, 1998).

[21] Alan Wakefield and Simon Moody, *Under the Devil's Eye: The British Military Experience in Macedonia 1915-18* (Stroud: Sutton Publishing, 2004).

[22] Richard C. Hall, *Balkan Breakthrough: The Battle of Dobro Pole 1918* (Bloomington: Indiana University Press, 2010).

[23] Milne was promoted to General in July 1918.

[24] Graham Nicol, *Uncle George: Biography of Field Marshal Lord Milne of Salonika and Rubislaw* (London: Reedminster Publications Ltd, 1976).

[25] In this paper, Milne usefully sets out his opinions of the causes of victory and the lessons to be drawn therefrom.

[26] Kings College London, Liddell Hart Centre for Military Archives (LHCMA), Field Marshal George F. Milne Papers,

[27] Harry Collinson Owen, *Salonica and After: The sideshow that ended the war* (London: Hodder & Stoughton, 1919).

[28] Collinson Owen, pp. v-vi. The author's note is a form of preface to the book.

[29] Henry C. Day, *Macedonian Memories* (London: H. Cranton, 1930).

[30] *The Mosquito*, December 1968.

[31] *The Mosquito*, September 1937.

[32] He was promoted to Marshal of France in 1921.

[33] *The Times*, 10 November 1928.

[34] Falls, II, 289-92, expands on these opportunities.

[35] Falls, II, 351.

[36] David Dutton, 'France, England and the Politics of the Salonica Campaign' (unpublished doctoral thesis, University College London, 1975). Dutton is not surprised that, with such uneven cooperation between the allies, the Salonika expedition emerged as one of the least fruitful exercises in the Allied direction of the war.

[37] TNA, WO 106/1385/008, Report on the situation in the Balkans, 3 August 1918.

[38] TNA, WO 106/1385/020, Milne to War Office, 22 July 1918.

[39] Falls, II, 323-4. The translated instructions of 24 July are reproduced as an Appendix.

[40] Falls, II, 325-6. The telegrams are reproduced as an Appendix.

[41] Falls, II, 111. The attendees at this meeting, and the sequence of events are laid out here.

[42] Falls, II, 116.

[43] Hall, p. 144.

[44] Wakefield & Moody, p. 213.

[45] Lieutenant-General H. F. M Wilson, not to be confused with Sir Henry Wilson, the CIGS, or Lieutenant-Colonel (later Field Marshal 1st Baron) Henry 'Jumbo' Maitland Wilson, his nephew.

[46] Falls, II, 207 and Appendix 17.

[47] Falls, II, 186, gives the complete analysis.

[48] Lieutenant-Colonel Daniel Burges was wounded three times, left behind with other casualties and taken prisoner. He survived.

[49] Falls, II, 190.

[50] Charles Packer, *Return to Salonika* (London: Cassell, 1964), p. 148.

[51] TNA, ADM 137/2180. A telegram sent to the Admiralty on 2 November 1918 from Vice-Admiral Gough-Calthorpe, the Chief British negotiator with the Turks, records the French objections to their exclusion. The Admiralty replied on 4 November that he had acted quite rightly in excluding those representatives.

[52] Collinson Owen, p. 235.

[53] *The Times* 23 January 1919.The report of General Milne was published in an abridged form, sometime after it was dated.

[54] Collinson Owen, pp. 244-5.

[55] Palmer, pp. 210-1.

[56] Hall, pp. 143-4.

[57] Stevenson, p. 147.

[58] An Unprofessional Soldier, 'I saw the Futile Massacre at Doiran', in *The Great War: I Was There: Issue 46*, ed. by John Hammerton (London: Amalgamated Press, 1938).

[59] *The Mosquito*, September 1937. Letter to the Editor from H.F. Heywood.

[60] LHCMA, Field Marshal George F. Milne Papers, Box 4. It is a matter for conjecture of what Milne and his army made of the

messages from the Superintendent of the Government Rolling Mills in Southampton or the Hon. Secretary of the Unionist Labour Party.

[61] TNA, WO 106/1367/147, General Franchet d'Espérey's weekly report to the War Minister, 23 September 1918.

[62] TNA, WO 106/1367/148, General Franchet d'Espérey's weekly report to the War Minister, 30 September 1918.

[63] Nicol, pp. 173-81, summarises these exchanges.

[64] *The Times*, 23 January 1919.

[65] LHCMA, Field Marshal George F. Milne Papers, Box 12. Paper dated 6 March 1939, given in Montevideo at the invitation of the Minister of Defence of Uruguay.

[66] *The Times*, 8 November 1918.

[67] TNA, Lloyd George MSS F/52/2/43, Clemenceau to Lloyd George, translation dated 25 October 1918, but the original letter in French is dated 21 October.

[68] TNA, Lloyd George MSS F/50/3/39, Lloyd George to Clemenceau, 25 October 1918. The exchange, somewhat disappointingly, ceases when a British Admiral, Vice-Admiral Gough-Calthorpe, concluded the armistice with the Turks that was signed on 30 October. The French (and Italians) were excluded from this negotiation.

[69] The Bulgarian Armistice Convention of 29 September 1918 is reproduced in full in the *American Journal of International Law*, 13/4 (1919), 402-4.

[70] Stevenson p. 147.

[71] The memorial to the BSF at Doiran in Greece commemorates the 1,979 members who fell in Macedonia who have no known grave. The nearby cemetery contains 1,338 burials of which 449 are unidentified. The graves are almost entirely those who fell in the fighting at Doran in April and May 1917, and September 1918. The 1918 battlefield site is just over the border, in the Former Yugoslav Republic of Macedonia (FYROM).

[72] *The Times*, 10 November 1928.

[73] Wakefield and Moody, pp. 237-40. This appendix lists the Order of Battle showing the BSF at its strongest in March 1917.

[74] TNA, CAB 24/12/006, Report on the Withdrawal of the British from Salonika, by Field-Marshal W. R. Robertson, CIGS, dated 1 May 1917.

[75] George Ward Price, *The Story of the Salonica Army* (London: Hodder & Stoughton, 1918), pp. 2-3.

[76] The road from Salonika to Seres was the most important for the BSF as it led to the Struma sector, and there was no railway.

[77] In Falls, I, 274, Falls describes four railway lines. The three referred to by Ward Price were those that ran in the direction of the front.

[78] Falls, II, 70-5. The issues were discussed between Milne, Guillaumat and the Military Representatives to the War Council.

[79] *The Mosquito*, September 1945. Quote from Milne's last address to the Salonika Reunion Association.

[80] The modern road is now a fine metalled surface.

[81] TNA, CAB 24/9/48. Report on the Situation at Salonika by Field Marshal W. R. Robertson CIGS, dated 2 April 1917.

[82] The Doiran front was served by one of the existing railway lines.

[83] Collinson Owen, p. 47.

[84] Falls, II, 281.

[85] Collinson Owen, p. 181.

[86] Collinson Owen, pp. 181-2.

[87] Vincent Julian Seligman, *The Salonica Side-Show* (London: G. Allen & Unwin, 1919).

[88] Seligman, pp. 25-7.

[89] Shipping matters and the danger posed by enemy submarines will be considered in Chapter Three.

[90] Ward Price, p. 254.

[91] LHCMA, Field-Marshal George F. Milne Papers, Box 12. Paper, dated 6 March 1939, given in Montevideo.

[92] The Vardar line branched, one line going north to Skopje and beyond, and the other going east to Constantinople via Doiran. The Monastir line led up to the French sector. Milne does not refer to the line that led south, eventually connecting to Athens, presumably because it did not lead to a front.

[93] TNA, CAB 25/34. Report by the Military Mission to Salonika, 18 June 1918.

[94] Falls, II, 17-19.

[95] Falls, II, 285-7, summarises in detail the activities in respect of drilling for water.

[96] This knowledge subsequently enabled the Greeks to deal with an estimated one million refugees who arrived in the Macedonia area in 1923 as a result of population displacements arising from the Greco-Turkish war.

[97] TNA, CAB 24/12/006, Report to the War Cabinet by Field Marshal W. R. Robertson, CIGS, 1 May 1917.

[98] This process had previously been implemented on the Western Front, for the same manpower shortage reasons.

[99] The political history of Greece during this period was most intricate, and is beyond the scope of this dissertation.

[100] Falls, II, 360-1.

[101] Falls, II, 65.

[102] Falls, II, 67.

[103] William G. Macpherson and Thomas J. Mitchell, *History of the Great War Medical Services,* 4 vols (London: HMSO, 1931), I, 95.

[104] Macpherson & Mitchell, IV, 90-103.

[105] Collinson Hall, p. 190. The 'Y' Scheme is also considered in Chapter Three.

[106] Falls, I, 268.

[107] More details can be found on http://scottishwomenshospitals.co.uk

[108] Collinson Owen, p. 104. Quotation from the Greek journal, *Phos.* Owen considers the flowery language used is natural to a Greek writing with a pen dipped in enthusiasm.

[109] Collinson Owen, p. 144.

[110] *The Times,* 8 November 1918 (letter dated 24 October 1918).

[111] *The Mosquito*, September 1945.

[112] Rachel Richardson, 'Home Away from the Home Front: The British in the Balkans in the Great War' (unpublished doctoral thesis, Birkbeck College, London, 2014).

[113] Richardson, pp. 197-200.

[114] TNA, CAB 24/6/005, Report by Liaison Officer between the War Office and Salonika on the French attitude towards Greece, and their relations to the BSF, dated 10 February 1917. In this particular report, the Greeks are quoted as remonstrating with the French for

not formulating their demands in a courteous matter, unlike the British.

[115] TNA, CAB 24/47/072, Eighth visit of Lt-Colonel EA Plunkett, General Staff, to the BSF, dated 24 March 1918.

[116] TNA, CAB 24/6/013, BSF Summary of Information January 1917, dated 1 February 1917.

[117] TNA, CAB 24/51/066, BSF Summary of Information April 1918, dated 5 May 1918.

[118] The airship was caught in a searchlight and engaged by the battleship HMS *Agamemnon,* who scored the hit that forced the airship down.

[119] Wakefield and Moody, pp. 183-8.

[120] TNA, CAB 24/51/066, Report to the CIGS, 1 May 1918.

[121] Collinson Owen, p. 285.

[122] Falls, II, 207.

[123] Collinson Owen, p. 286.

[124] Seligman, p. 135.

[125] Collinson Owen, p. 287.

[126] *The Times,* 23 January 1919.

[127] TNA, WO 106/1367/148.

[128] TNA, CAB 24/9/048, Situation at Salonika.

[129] TNA, CAB 24/12/006, Withdrawal of the British from Salonika, report dated 1 May 1917.

[130] Eric Grove, 'Salonika and Macedonia: The Vital Maritime Dimension' (unpublished paper given at the International Conference on The Salonika Front in World War One, Thessaloniki, 22-24 October 2015).

[131] E. Keble Chatterton, *Seas of Adventures* (London: Hurst & Blackett, 1936), pp. 263-6.

[132] TNA, ADM 116/1420, Memorandum by Ministry of Shipping, 10 January 1918.

[133] TNA, ADM 137/1575, Memorandum by Calthorpe dated 7 February 1918. Remarks on the situation in the Aegean.

[134] TNA, ADM 116/1807, Memorandum by Geddes, 15 February 1918. The *Goeben* remained in the Turkish Navy until decommissioned in 1950.

[135] TNA, ADM 116/1809, Calthorpe to Geddes, 4 September 1918. This letter contains an analysis of declining tonnages of lost shipping from May to August 1918.

[136] TNA, ADM 137/1580, Milne to War Office, 28 April 1918.

[137] TNA, ADM 116/1810, Admiralty Memorandum to War Cabinet, 12 October 1918.

[138] Falls, II, 34.

[139] Seligman, p. 254.

[140] Collinson Owen, p. 190.

[141] *Hansard*, 108, c1834W, Commons Debate of 24 July 1918.

[142] *Hansard*, 109, cc636-7W, Commons Debate of 1 August 1918.

[143] Eric Grove, 'Salonika and Macedonia' (unpublished paper, given at the International Conference on The Salonika Front in World War One, Thessaloniki, 22-24 October 2015).

[144] Falls, II, 118-19.

[145] Paul G. Halpern, *The Royal Navy in the Mediterranean, 1915-18* (Aldershot: Temple Smith, 1987), pp. 467-9. Letter from Commander G. C. Dickens to Captain K. G. B. Dewar, 9 May 1918.

[146] Arthur James Mann, *The Salonika Front* (London: A & C Black, 1920), p. 168.

[147] *The Times*, 10 November 1928.

[148] Nicol, p. 189

[149] Edmund Allenby was created a Field-Marshal and Viscount in 1919. Frederick, Earl of Cavan was promoted to General in 1921, and subsequently became a Field-Marshal in 1932.

[150] *Hansard*, vol 119 cc904-5W. Commons debate of 11 August 1919.

[151] He rose to become Field-Marshal Lord Milne of Salonika and Rubislaw.

[152] D Dieterich, *Weltkreigsende an Der Mazedonischen Front* (Berlin: Gerhard Stalling, 1928).

[153] Ludendorff, II, 714-15.

[154] Pogradec was considered a minor Franco-Serbian operation in September 1917, on the extreme left flank. Skra di Legen, in May 1918, was a French and Greek operation.

[155] The exchanges between the two are discussed in Chapter One.

[156] As translated from Clemenceau's newspaper, *L'homme Enchaîné*, 6 May 1917.

[157] Seligman, p. 254-5.

[158] Ludendorff, II, 716.

[159] Collinson Owen, Title Page.

[160] Collinson Owen, pp. 274-6.

[161] LHCMA, Field Marshal George F. Milne Papers, Box 12. Paper dated 6 March 1939, given in Montevideo at the invitation of the Minister of Defence of Uruguay.

[162] *The Mosquito*, December 1968 edition. The quotation is from Churchill, *The World Crisi*s, III, published in 1929.

[163] Palmer, p. 239.

[164] Palmer, p. 243.

[165] Stevenson, p. xvi.

[166] Stevenson, pp. 509-10.

[167] Hall, pp. 143-4.

[168] Stevenson, p.147.

[169] Falls, II, 324.

[170] Falls, II, 327-33. The translated full orders are reproduced here as an Appendix.

[171] *Chicago Daily Tribune*, 1 October 1918. A copy of the front page is on page ii of this dissertation.

Printed in Great Britain
by Amazon

57141582R00116